# A JOURNEY OF INSIGHTS

# A JOURNEY OF INSIGHTS

## LESSONS *in* LEADERSHIP *and* LEGACY

JAMES G. ELLIS

LYONS PRESS

*Essex, Connecticut*

LP
LYONS PRESS

An imprint of The Globe Pequot Publishing Group, Inc.
64 S Main St.
Essex, CT 06426
www.globepequot.com



British Library Cataloguing in Publication Information available

Library of Congress Cataloging-in-Publication Data available
ISBN 9781493096084 (cloth) | ISBN 9781493096091 (epub)

# Contents

*With deep love, thanks, and appreciation*
*To*
*My wife, Gail,*
*and*
*Our kids: Brian, Carrie, Jessica, Tiffany, Rob*
*For all the life experiences that allowed me*
*to write this book and share my thoughts*

# Foreword

In this delightful and instructive book, Jim Ellis offers valuable career and life advice through the stories of his interactions with people he has known and worked with along the way. Ellis's own experiences as entrepreneur, educator, civic leader, and family man give him a keen sense of the most important aspects of building a successful and fulfilling life, and he draws on his experience and relationships to convey powerful and useful lessons. From his dozens of interactions with presidents, military leaders, students, businesspeople, family, and friends, Jim shares compelling stories that we can apply daily.

Ellis is an accessible writer for readers of all kinds, his ability to listen and learn—to pay attention to people of all ages and stages—helps him develop authentic relationships with humility and wisdom and allows him to glean practical wisdom that he shares.

Jim knows the importance of classroom learning and that every level of schooling is an enduring investment in ourselves. Classrooms are the places we are exposed to experts and practitioners in an environment created to support students and their interests. But classrooms are not the only places where we learn. In this day of rapid change and transformation brought on by technological advances, changing demographics, shifting priorities, and new opportunities, relationships and connections are at least of equal value. Jim understands and elevates the value of both parts of becoming "educated" and ready to live a fulfilling life.

These days we hear a lot about "storytelling" even if sometimes we are not always sure about the value of it. One thing we know for sure, however, is that investing in and maximizing our own relationships is important and rewarding. Through Jim's ability to listen, observe, question, and glean, he provides a model for how we might enrich our own connections and relationships.

Ellis discusses key milestones—like deciding on how best to develop your education and skills, how to chart your professional course, and how to navigate change. He is honest in his telling of his own course corrections and shares his insights with grace and humility. Jim's warmth and character transcend the page, making the reader feel as if they have a new friend in Jim.

Through a series of thought-provoking questions that follow each chapter, Ellis demonstrates his superb teaching skills and opens a window in each of us to reflect and grow. When was the last time you asked yourself the serious questions that guide a life? Jim prompts us to do that in a fun and practical way, which makes this book both inspiring and useful.

As one of many thousands who has had the privilege knowing and working with Jim, I can personally attest to his ability to bring out the best in people. I have seen him tackle and embrace disappointment and success. He and I have shared experiences with the challenges of higher education administration, and his candor and integrity are refreshing as he reflects on those experiences. Higher education needs more leaders like Jim demonstrating to students how to navigate these issues now.

As a teacher, mentor, colleague, and friend, Jim is generous in his approach. He understands the responsibility and privilege of the opportunities he has had and pays it forward so we can all benefit. Thank you, Jim, for this fun and insightful read.

Margaret Spellings
Former United States Secretary of Education
Former President, University of North Carolina System
CEO, Bipartisan Policy Center

# Introduction

## Charlottesville, VA—August 30, 2008

It was hot, humid, and almost airless at Thomas Jefferson's university for the annual gridiron competition between the University of Virginia's Cavaliers and the Trojans of the University of Southern California. Nevertheless, most of the Virginia gentlemen in the stands were wearing coats and ties, continuing a long-standing UVA tradition. Women were properly dressed as well. What a dramatic difference from the T-shirts and flip-flops worn by the USC students at homes games in California. The game's result, USC 52, UVA 7, did nothing to improve the Cavaliers' collective mood or comfort.

For this annual rite, I brought some of my board members along with their spouses and friends to the football game and suggested to **Bob Bruner**, dean of UVA's Darden Graduate School of Business, that we meet the day before with a similar group of leaders from his business school to discuss the decisions business schools would confront in the future. I stood to gain a lot from the discussion since I had been dean of USC's Marshall School of Business only since April 2007. Bruner, on the other hand, was a well-credentialed pro among business school deans, having held the post since 2005 shortly after he published a commanding textbook, *Applied Mergers and Acquisitions*, which sold 1.3 million copies over time. Bob undertook the planning of our joint session with gusto. He prepared a presentation on the critical decisions that business school deans would face and asked the "class" to opine on those issues. The meeting simulated our classroom "case-study" discussions, asking the "students" the basic question in every business school classroom: What would you decide in this situation? Bob was asking us what should graduate business schools do to stay vital in a changing world.

In other words, what do deans and trustees need to do if they want to improve their standing in the ranking of educational institutions and anticipate the needs of the future employers of their students?

One of the members of Marshall's board was **Fred Price**, then a managing principal with the Sander O'Neill investment banking firm (bought by Piper Jaffray in 2020). Fred brought along his friend of the same first name, **Fred Ridley**, a commercial real estate attorney with the international firm of Foley and Lardner, who was interested in being part of the meeting. It was astonishingly helpful to have someone there with no connection to either business school. In fact, Ridley's presence probably caused us to focus more intensely on what was being suggested and discussed.

With a stranger in the room—one as smart and collegial as Ridley, who later became chair of Augusta National Golf Club—nobody could fall back on professional or tired, shorthand explanations. Ridley's presence brought a higher level of collaborative thought out of us. We could see firsthand the value of having an outsider participate in critical analysis.

Some of the major challenges facing us—such as how to develop a global reach and consciousness—were apparent. But what were the correct strategies to use? Some schools had gone the brick-and-mortar route; Duke for instance, had built an appendage of its North Carolina business school in China. But a number of us at USC felt that it would be smarter to develop multiple international programs aimed at building relationships with many different nations rather than being confined to one or two campus facilities in particular countries. We had seen that commercial attitudes toward certain countries could change; Japan, for example, had been the darling of the business world during the 1980s but its allure as a place to learn forward-leaning business practices began fading by the 1990s. Some emerging or rapidly mutating economies in Latin America, Southeast Asia, and the oil-soaked Middle East principalities could offer American business schools a duality of opportunities—both places to recruit students who would enrich our classrooms stateside and foreign partners for reciprocal programs. In the years following our Charlottesville exploration of the globalization of our universities, USC built out a variety of new international initiatives, aggressively developing a reputation among educators for innovation and muscular bonding with its intensely loyal alumni body, a natural employer pool for its graduates.

Much of the inspiration for this growth emanated from **Steven Sample**, USC's tenth president from 1991 to 2010. An engineer by training and inventor of some significant patents in microwaves, Steve approached his role at the university as an engineer would—identifying the problems and opportunities and setting about to solve issues by taking advantage of what he saw in front of him. He overcame the risks faced by all university presidents with the power of his vision. When he began his tenure, USC was primarily a regional research university languishing as #41 in the US News and World Report rankings with a reputation of being an easy school for admissions (70 percent acceptance rate) and graduation—a school of endless fraternity parties, athletics, and affluent, vapid students. Wags called USC the "university of spoiled children."

Sample's genius was to drive the change that would eventually lift the university to national stature and #23 in the US News and World Report rankings, engineering a transformation by providing a strong, consistent message of aiming high and not avoiding risks. The marketing campaign for the Admissions department used the tagline "Let Us Spoil Your Children with a Great Education," turning a liability into an asset. And with the help of his handpicked provost and eventual successor as president, **Chrysostomas Loizos "Max" Nikias**, he raised enormous amounts of money. When the inventor of the diabetic pump, Alfred Mann, offered $100 million to UCLA with conditions that UCLA did not like, Sample went after the opportunity and bagged the $100 million for USC. Similarly, when Nikias landed a $52 million donation from the cofounder of Qualcomm, Andrew Viterbi, and named the engineering school after him, USC became one of three universities in the country to rank among the top five largest university fundraisers for five consecutive years—the others being Harvard and Stanford. Sample's vision, imparted to all of his deans, was simple but powerful: "Continue to deliver your message over and over again—your constituents will not tire of hearing it—and be patient. Donors have their own rhythm and reasons for giving which you cannot force. Your successors may reap the benefit of your work."

USC's success under inspired leadership could easily be a case study itself in a business school course on entrepreneurship or managing change. In addition to the opening of new research centers, a long and sustained building boom, which added 25 percent more student housing and wiped away nearby distressed neighborhoods, hiring sprees of topflight professors, and the record-shattering improvements in student applications, financial aid, diversity statistics, and the recruitment of international students, there would be the challenges that accompany success: parents trying to buy admissions for their children and misbehaving academics who if they'd read the memo from on high had not absorbed it. The darker moments would be dealt with surgically and usually adroitly because the new and improved USC with its impressive board of trustees of more than forty-five accomplished and generous benefactors was strong and stable enough to handle them.

This book draws upon the lessons I learned while a teacher and dean of USC's Marshall School of Business and the lessons I absorbed during my preceding years at the University of New Mexico, at Harvard Business School, and in business. In trying to plot the road map for a successful business life, my stories attempt to show illustratively the secrets or ingredients of how students, as well as business schools, can prosper. At the core of my message is the central theme that listening to voices around you throughout life is the key to success. In essence, ears can speak louder than voices.

The value of listening was shown to me dramatically by one of my professors, **Anthony Athos**, during my second year in graduate school. Athos taught classes in interpersonal and organizational behavior and was amazing in the classroom. In 1966, he was on the cover of *Time* magazine, being recognized as one of America's "great teachers" by that publication. As students in his classroom, we knew we were in the presence of a true icon in his world.

Tony was strong in his belief that a good leader is a GREAT listener, and he spent a considerable amount of time talking about that. It was so important that he asked us for a demonstration of our listening skills as the final examination in his course. And what an exam it was.

We were to call upon someone we knew, but not too well, to come to campus where we could interview them. A fellow classmate would sit quietly during the interview and grade how well we listened. We were only allowed to ask one question in a forty-five-minute interview, and then we could repeat the last phrase or sentence the interviewee had uttered, or just say "Ahhh" or "Oh?" or "Uh-huh." We literally were not to talk during this time.

I had invited Bill Townsend to be my interviewee. He was the brother of a woman I was dating at the time. He came to campus, and we sat in a small carrel in the hallway, secluded, with my classmate/grader in attendance as well. Perhaps I hadn't explained that situation to Bill too thoroughly, because the first thing he said once he took a seat was, "Jim, what is this all about?" I answered with the one statement I was allowed, which I hoped would trigger our interview: "Bill, tell me about you." That was ALL I could say. Bill proceeded to tell me that he had grown up in a Midwestern city, but subsequently left to come to the Northeast in search of a job. As I repeated the last phrase he had said or egged him on with a series of "Ahhs" and "Ohhs," he opened up about so many things that I could barely keep up.

By the end of the required forty-five minutes, I had learned that he did not like his dad, was jealous of his much brighter sister, had no self-esteem, had a drinking problem, had a drug problem, and in general was a mess! I cannot tell you how many times I wanted to come over the table and tell him, "You need to get help—NOW!" but I couldn't, and I didn't.

At the end of the "interview," I was sweating profusely—yes, imagine breaking a sweat from just listening? Though I had barely spoken, my throat felt so dried and tight that I was in desperate need of a drink of water. As I excused myself and headed for the nearest drinking fountain, Bill turned to my classmate and proclaimed, "He's a great guy, isn't he?" He knew nothing about me from that interview, and yet thought enough to make that statement. The power of listening had proven itself to me in two ways: I had learned A LOT about Bill, and he came away knowing I cared about him because I had taken the time to listen. Every time I have used this technique to gather information, I am floored by how much I truly learn. People are willing to speak to others if others are willing to listen.

I started teaching at age fifty. I don't think I could have done it any earlier in my life. I needed time to build financial security, so that I would never feel I was teaching just for a paycheck. More importantly, I needed time and experience to top off a storage tank full of stories to share with my students. I didn't quite understand the crucial importance of those stories when I began teaching. There was a theory that needed to be explained in the classroom and curricula that needed to be covered and lesson plans to be followed. But I quickly found that my stories—my life experiences—easily ran in parallel with the theory-based lessons and would in fact bring those lessons to life better than any readings from a textbook. Our most powerful moments of education arrive through the understanding of a story, or through the discovery of a story behind the dry facts. I didn't always know what personal story would work in a particular class—they tended to pop out extemporaneously. Thus, this book cascades through many, many stories in order to illuminate how students, and people in general, can thrive. The closing of each chapter will pose thought exercises for readers to ask and consider in their own situation.

One personal story—from my youth—stands out among all the lessons I've learned from countless people along the way. It provides the bedrock foundation for success in any business school and beyond. It took place at the San Francisco airport back in 1959 when air travel was a big deal and an airport, an exciting place.

I was twelve years old at the time with my father, and I could barely contain my excitement. I kept running ahead of him to scout out more of the terminal, then running back to him so I could report what I'd observed. This worked fine until I attempted to sprint through a more crowded section of one passageway and barreled straight into a well-dressed stranger—a handsome man in a dark, pin-striped suit. I hit him pretty hard, but as any kid might, I just bounced off and kept going as he caromed off the wall behind him. I went a little farther ahead, then waited for my father to catch up with me. When he did, he said that he'd seen me bump into the stranger, and he suggested I backtrack and apologize.

My father seemed serious enough about this request that I didn't consider putting up any resistance. I headed in the direction of where the stranger had hit the wall and quickly spotted him there, now talking to some men. He had a great head of hair that was hard to miss. I worked my way to him, and he looked my way, a bit surprised to see me again. I told him, somewhat sheepishly, that I was very sorry I had run into him, and I was sorry if I hurt him—I understood that the collision was totally my fault. I suppose I thought that this grown-up might express some anger or annoyance with a kid like me, but he just smiled. "You didn't hurt me," he said warmly. "But the fact that you would come back to me and offer a genuine apology means a great deal. If you will continue to take responsibility at the appropriate times in your life, that's good enough for me. And I am not hurt. Thank you."

I certainly hadn't expected to be thanked by someone I had plowed into, so I thanked him in return and headed back toward my father, feeling my spirits lifted. At my father's side, he asked if I knew who I'd just been talking to. I told him I didn't. How could I? I was only twelve, and the only person I had ever known to wear a suit was Dad.

"He's probably going to be our next president," my father said. "That's **Senator John F. Kennedy** from Massachusetts." I looked back one more time at the friendly stranger. He stood with one hand in a suit coat pocket, still talking to a few people. As far as I could tell, he didn't have any security around him, but there was still something about him that made him the center of attention, even in a busy airport terminal. I thought about the way he looked and the understanding he'd expressed in his words. He sure seemed presidential to me.

I think back to my sudden, impactful encounter with JFK because it's an early, dramatic example of what's become a guiding principle for me: Life lessons, large and small, are available from the people all around us. At the airport, my father and a president-to-be taught me something about the importance of taking responsibility for one's actions, and the power of a sincere apology. Throughout all our lives, similarly effective lessons may come from our family, friends, classmates, work colleagues, and even strangers, well dressed or not. We simply need to learn how to be open to such lessons when they present themselves.

We're not all running for president (thank goodness), but we can all aspire to the quality of leadership, in our workplace or our lives outside of work, and we gradually build our own leadership "portfolio" through learnings from others, beginning with our parents. Some of those learnings come directly at us and have an immediate, powerful effect on us, just as they were meant to do (Don't touch a hot stove!). We may learn from those who are of equal status in our school, work, or social circles, or we may be fortunate enough to receive wisdom from those who are further along in their life's journey. We may also be surprised to be schooled by those we didn't expect to learn from. However, when the lessons arrive, and whoever they come from, we need to pay heed to these learnings and store them in a way that allows us to draw upon them as part of the decision process in our daily lives.

The chapters that follow flesh out the corners of my life but are easily stated. I grew up in Albuquerque, New Mexico, attended the University of New Mexico, then earned my MBA at Harvard Business School. With that degree in hand, I relocated to Southern California (partly because SoCal offered greater weather for golfing than Cambridge did). I embarked on a business career in which I held executive positions at such venerable (now defunct) retail firms as The Broadway department stores and Miller's Outpost. After several years in the retail world, I transitioned into entrepreneurship and bought a company that sold men's and women's apparel directly to military bases.

Eventually I sold that company and was "between jobs," as they say, when I met the love of my life, Gail, on a blind date. I had it in my head that the right woman for me would be single and childless and live in my town (San Diego at the time). Gail was divorced, had four children, and lived in Chicago. However, our second date was a weeklong ski trip to Vail, and at the end of the week, I asked her to marry me! I knew it was right, and it has been—for over forty years! And the four kids? They are four of my closest friends today. As is their youngest brother—a fifth child whom Gail and I had together.

The expertise I'd picked up in global commerce with the retail chains paid off when automotive giant Porsche recruited me to be the president/CEO of the American distribution wing of Porsche Design, overseeing all the nonautomotive apparel and merchandise related to the brand. My success there led to a crossroads—moving any higher up the corporate ladder would require my family to relocate to Europe. We preferred to stay in Southern California, especially since we had five kids in five different schools!

So, we spent the next seven years buying, selling, and operating some nine different companies across the fields of manufacturing, distribution, and retail—enterprises ranging from a chain of sock stores to sheet metal fabrication and ceramic paint factories.

If the first big lesson I learned was "Watch where you are going in airports," the second one was "Be ready for change." The greatest change in my career path came about by way of a blank sheet of paper, and I am thrilled that I was ready for it.

The Young Presidents' Organization is a global leadership community of chief executives who've achieved that position before the age of forty-five. YPO currently has more than thirty thousand members in over 140 countries. I became a member in 1987, and while I've always found the group's large-scale, invitation-only gatherings to be useful and extremely educational, my membership's greatest benefit has been the opportunity to be part of highly confidential small-group forums. In the small-group meetings, otherwise "together" bosses can admit to all their fears and doubts, as well as receive support and advice from fellow bosses who know exactly what those fears and doubts feel like. Personal problems can be aired, triumphs can be celebrated, and career decisions can be workshopped in strictest confidence.

In 1996, my family was quite happy, and my career was running strong. But in one of those small-group forums, some YPO friends posed an intriguing question to me: If I had a blank sheet of paper on which I could write what I wanted from the next twenty-five years of my life, what would I fill that blank paper with? It had been a long time since I felt like I had a clean sheet of paper to work with, what with the burden of mortgages, tuitions, and maintaining my family's lifestyle at a certain level. But I thought hard about the question, and my answer was that I would like to spend those coming years sharing the experiences of being in business with those who might be following me, through combinations of speaking, writing, consulting, or teaching.

One of the members had a response that was simple and to the point.

"Do it," he said.

"That's a nice idea, but how do I do it?" I asked.

"You'll figure it out," someone else replied.

The blank piece of paper might have remained a thought exercise, but shortly after that meeting I had breakfast with an old friend who mentioned that the University of Southern California was looking for a marketing professor and that he thought of me. Normally, I might have shrugged off this bit of information for change. I connected with the appropriate offices at USC and by January 1997—after twenty-seven years in the business world—I was starting my life on a fresh piece of paper.

This book celebrates the many people who shared their insights with me, and now I share their gifts with you. Of course, my life experiences have also included encounters with negative and unhelpful people—let's call them jerks—but I've chosen not to waste precious energy cataloging them in these pages. Somewhere along the line I learned the very helpful trick of dismissing those who negatively impact me, and not allowing them to exist in my memories. The chapters that follow are organized thematically around such topics as family, career, education, and passion. Within each chapter, I relay stories, experiences, and connections to people who can teach you, as they did me, about the business of life.

# Chapter 1

# A Dean's Story

## *The Cold Car Hood*

You are entitled to know some things about the person dispensing the lessons in this book, so here is my story. Whether happy or not, all families exert a strong influence on the adults we become. We first develop a sense of values and principles in the family setting, either by adopting the values we see demonstrated by family members or by figuring out our own moral code in response to family values we don't feel comfortable with. Whether our families influence us positively or negatively, directly or indirectly, the impacts of these earliest relationships are powerful and enduring.

As for my own family background, I was born in Tacoma, Washington, and spent a few childhood years in Northern and Southern California. My father, George Ellis, was a banker who had developed an interesting philosophy in terms of business success: He felt he had to move to a new bank every couple of years to move up the corporate ladder. By the time I started ninth grade, my family settled in Albuquerque, and that is the place I really consider to be my early home. In Albuquerque, my father earned his way to the top of the ladder. He became a bank president there, so no further moves were necessary (or so I thought—he'd go on to be a bank president in Los Angeles and San Diego as well).

My earliest impression of what the work world looked like was shaped in my father's bank. He would take me down to his office every Saturday when he would put in an extra day's work and he'd say, "Pick a desk to sit at. Who do you want to be today? Do you want to be the vice president? Do you want to sit in the teller cage? Do you want to be a loan officer?" I'd pick a desk and sit there feeling like a big shot doing vocabulary homework at a vice president's desk while my dad worked in his office at the president's desk. When he got enough of his work done, we would go out and play golf together or go to a baseball game, and that's when he would shift from being a mentor to being a dad. But he showed me, without having to say much about it, that Saturday was a workday. If you got work done on a Saturday, you really earned your fun.

My father was a good, solid business guy who based everything on relationships. To that end his office, as the CEO of a multibranch bank in San Diego, was in the middle of the lobby—a desk, chairs, and a couch surrounded by glass walls. He wanted the customers of his largest branch to see that he was there every day, protecting their assets. On the regular workdays that I was able to spend in the bank, I always enjoyed watching my father in action. I remember one day a guy came through the bank and waved a check at my dad. "Well, George—another ten million dollars!" he said. "That's great," my father responded. Then he turned to me and said, "See that man with that check? He's about to put ten million dollars into his personal checking account."

"Where does he get that kind of money?" I asked.

My dad said, "Well, he's the largest condom maker in the world."

"Really?"

"Plenty of people buy them," my dad said. "Somebody's got to make them."

Dad was a crucial guide to me when it came time for me to make some education and career choices, and I've come to see him as one of the great mentors in my life, providing a gold standard for how to be a husband and father, as well as how to conduct myself as a businessperson. My sense of values and principles was also greatly affected by my mother—a deeply religious woman who took great pride in the home she provided for me, my brother, and my sister. She was one of the smartest people I've ever met and had been the valedictorian of her high school and college classes (the family used to joke that my mother had never received a B in her life, and while the same was true of my father, he was on the other end of the grading curve). She was an amazing woman—the rock who provided the foundation for our family life.

It goes without saying that families are complicated. As a dean of students, I've seen a very wide range of family dynamics, from those families that functioned as a nexus of love and support to those that were thoroughly toxic and destructive. Your family relationships can be an enduring source of strength in your life, but if that's not the case for you, you can find the support and constancy that a family should have provided in the other relationships you develop throughout your education and career. A lot of us get two families in our lifetime: the one we're born into and the one we create with a spouse. As it turned out, my career decision to become a dean affected my wife's life as much as it did mine. Together we hosted enough cocktail and dinner parties at our home that we could have been running a banquet hall. By my count, Gail and I entertained about four thousand people over the time I was in the job. For me, being a dean, and doing the job well, required two people. So often I relied on Gail's input or counted on her at dinners when we'd split up in order to meet twice as many people. Many times, she first heard things from students that they wanted me to know but might not have told me directly.

One evening, I witnessed the same kind of spousal support that Gail offered me, with the spouse in question being none other than the prime minister of the United Kingdom. **Theresa May** attended a dinner in London with her husband, Philip, who worked for the Capital Group, of which I was a board member. While talking in a small group with her, one would never have known she was leading a country fraught with concern about breaking away from the European Union. That was partly explained by her natural calm and poise. But more to the point, she was there that night to support her husband in his role with that investment firm, and that was it. No speech from her, no airs from her, no politics—just support from one family member for another. She knew all the responsibilities she carried as prime minister, but she was there that night as a loving partner to her husband, and nothing else mattered. So admirable. Nothing about the couple that night indicated that one of them was a head of state. There were a couple of "Protection Command" officers present, who were tasked with providing security for the couple, but they were so low-key as to be unnoticeable; it was impossible to tell who they were protecting.

Family bonds can add comfort and joy to our lives, but it is also a sad reality that once those bonds are established, the loss of a family member leaves us with almost imaginable heartache. At such times family support is critical.

In 1982, my cousin Kevin was on a camera safari in southern Africa after his college graduation. One particular day, as he and about ten other young people plus chaperones were preparing to leave the area around Victoria Falls in Zimbabwe, twelve rebel soldiers came out of the bush and stopped the travelers' truck. They took Kevin and the five boys in the group and sent the girls and chaperones down the road. That was the last time that anyone saw the boys. For three years, we did not know anything of the captured group's whereabouts. Kevin's father, my uncle **Bill Ellis**, talked to the State Department daily, trying to get whatever information might be available. He traveled to Africa numerous times at his own expense, asking questions, searching for his only son. There were purported sightings, but never verified. Those glimmers kept our hopes alive.

As we watched this terrible drama unfold on an almost hourly basis, we saw how my uncle Bill tirelessly worked every angle he knew to get to the truth. Finally, sadly, he found one of the rebel soldiers in jail, who explained that Kevin had been shot the day after he was captured, as he ran out to signal rescue planes flying overhead. It was so devastating to our family, but we had closure at last. I will never forget my uncle's determination to bring his son back.

**As I have said, family support is critical, always.**

Meeting **Queen Rania Al Abdullah** of Jordan was special for me, and she was surprisingly family oriented. She was going to be on a tour of the United States and agreed to accept my invitation to speak to a YPO group at The Greenbrier, a spectacular resort in the Allegheny Mountains of West Virginia. I had the pleasure to spend time with her before the event, and I remember thinking that she was someone who truly put the "majesty" in "Queen"—she was intelligent, beautiful, articulate, and unfailingly gorgeous. Her Highness had worked for both Citibank and Apple prior to her marriage to then-Prince Abdullah. She was well grounded in the tenets of business, and she brought those assets to the marriage, helping the destined king as he built the economy of his country. During the time our group spent with her, she talked about the coming of the digital economy and the value of technology to her country in a truly informed, insightful way—most impressive. She answered all the questions put to her calmly and in great depth, such that it was easy to see what a great partner she was to the ruler of the country.

She stressed that it was extremely important for the royal family to stay connected to the people they ruled. She told us about how her husband would make evening forays out into the capital city of Amman, disguised as a cab driver or an emergency room orderly. These excursions always made her nervous, but she appreciated that he wanted to hear directly from his people about what they thought of the monarchy and their rulers.

The only time that Rania did not seem calm was when she spoke of her young children. Then, she absolutely lit up with such a smile and such emotion that it was impossible not to see the joy she took in being a mother. She spoke at length about driving her four children to school each day—no matter what else was on her schedule, that part of her day was a given and not to be tampered with. She was clearly a proud mom who wanted to be with her children as much as possible as they grew up.

**Even with a kingdom to run, family time can be a top priority.**

The balance between family and career can be difficult to achieve, and the struggle to find that balance is often emotionally fraught and packed with logistical considerations.

In the cosmetics industry, **Michelle Taylor** was a rising star. She had received her degrees from UCLA and USC but knew that to be a success in that business, she needed to be in New York. So, off she went, where she had such roles as director of US marketing for Elizabeth Arden, VP of marketing for Chanel, senior vice president/general manager for Frédéric Fekkai, SVP of Lancôme, and finally, SVP of L'Oreal USA. Her achievements in her chosen field were stellar, but there was an issue that she needed to face. Michelle and her husband, Craig, had four sons. The couple quickly discovered that it is no easy feat to raise boys in New York, especially with one parent doing the bulk of the parenting and the other pursuing a demanding, fast-paced career. Michelle came to realize that, despite her career achievements, she would regret not being part of her sons' early years of development, and though Craig was a loving, terrific father, she feared her absence from the day-to-day life of her sons would impact them as well. The couple decided to leave the high-powered New York environment and move back to California.

Such decisions are faced by many couples with growing families. Do they continue on the career path to great financial and material success, or do they move into the most difficult job there is—that of parenting children full-time? There are many factors that come into play in such a decision, and both parents need to weigh in as the decision is made.

Michelle and Craig agreed that their first priority was to raise their children together. They worked hard with their four young men, and all of them turned out to be exceptional.

As the boys moved on into their adult lives, Michelle looked around for business opportunities for herself. She was able to find a myriad of job prospects and continued her career in California—it was a win for the family on all sides.

**Creating a healthy, happy family is the hardest—and most rewarding—job you'll ever have.**

I never looked at my father as being one of my mentors until I was way down the road in years. Typically, I'd say that parents and close family members do not make good mentors, as their main job is primarily to provide you with unconditional love and support. While there can certainly be great affection between a mentor and student, that relationship is a very different one than a family bond.

Sometimes, a mentor has to chastise you for doing something you should not have done, or be tough on you for a particular direction you are taking. While parents can do that, their perspective is likely to be complicated by the emotions and expectations of a family. Great mentors have a much better shot at remaining objective. It can be easier for them to let you set your own course, while they monitor and encourage your progress through it.

My dad was a very loving father, but perhaps because he was so used to thinking as a businessperson—he was able to split his attention toward me and take on the role of a mentor who was not just there as source of unconditional love. He flourished in the role of mentor, and the side of him that was a dad did not enter into the mentorship because he was able to think in a very compartmentalized way. That, in and of itself, is a pretty good lesson that I certainly took to heart through the years: Family and business are two separate things, so keep them separate. The further along I got in my academic career and then my business career, the more my father was able to serve as a mentor, because he knew I was really starting to understand what he was telling me. Watching the way he did business established a gold standard for me that I applied to every other boss I encountered and tried to embody when I became a boss myself.

My father came from a very modest background—his dad worked on the Milwaukee Road railway in a little town in western Montana. My dad learned his work ethic directly from his father. Dad's mom was one of the world's greatest penny-pinchers. Nothing got past her, and she held my grandfather to a very tight budget. As a young boy, Dad held many jobs to contribute to the family, and upon graduation from college and mustering out of the US Navy, he started a long, successful career in commercial banking. He ended up at the top of his field, but he worked very hard to get there.

My father had that strong work ethic, an infectious laugh, and a people-focused approach to business and leadership/management. Once he'd had enough success to savor some of the finer things in life, he developed a passion for golf. I had some success as a member of my high school and college golf teams and, for a while, imagined that my calling in life was to be a professional golfer. One of the most significant instances of mentorship my father provided me with was when he told me he didn't think I'd go very far as a pro golfer and that I should consider business school instead. That wasn't easy to hear, but I'd already had enough experience on the greens to know that there were people out there with a lot more natural talent than me and a lot more dedication to the sport as well. The mentor was right—golf has remained a passionate hobby, but it would not have been a successful career for me. Some other lessons my father passed on to me, either directly or by example: "You've got to work hard to earn what you're going to get out of life." Don't shy away from putting in the time and effort that's required of you. Clock-watchers don't get ahead in a business environment—success comes to those who do their tasks well.

*"Be the first person to get to work in the morning and be the last person to leave at night."*

Even as bank president Dad followed this dictum, and he used to say that he wanted to get the bank early enough so that the hood of his car would be cold by the time the second person got to work. During the first fifteen years of my career, I was single, so I could get to work at five o'clock in the morning and leave the office at ten o'clock at night and not worry about impacting anyone but me. And that was a positive. Had I been a father, it would have been very, very different.

*"Leave time in your day to talk to those around you."*

Creativity in business doesn't just happen at your desk—it may be sparked by random hallway conversations or discussions in the employee cafeteria. The other minds around you are a resource—use them.

*"Return all your phone calls before you go home that day."*

Dad was really amazing at doing this, showing those who called him that he cared enough about them to get back to them quickly. In today's world of never-out-of-touch texts/calls/emails/voicemails, it is more difficult to get back to everyone right away, but I try hard to get back to as many people as I can, at least to let them know I have received their message, which then gives me time to answer a bit later. There have been times in my career when I received an average of 300 emails a day—with the record being 875 in one day! I would answer as many of them as I could, typically leaving 50 emails unanswered every day, which gave me the opportunity to answer the 250 left over on Saturday and Sunday. If someone wants you for something, give them the courtesy of the response. Your priority is your team, and then your customers—you need to assume that the team is responding to customer requests too.

*"Don't ever lie to your banker."*

Be completely up front with them. During the difficult times in any business, there can be a great temptation to shave the truth a bit so that people don't see what is actually happening. Resist that temptation. Honesty is always the right way to go, even when it sends you down the harder path. In my father's role as a lender, he wanted to know where the bank stood with the customer and the loan. Every time the truth was not forthcoming, suspicions arose, as they should have. That is never good for an ongoing relationship.

Now, extend that advice to the arenas of a marriage or friendship or whatever relationship you have:

*"Don't lie."*

It does not work in the long run and certainly will never work once the other knows you have a propensity for doing it. Truth will always win out and should. Just face the music and take it from there—it makes it easier to keep your story straight, and you never have to remember what you said to whom.

The two significant women in my life have been my mother and my wife, and it is through them that I discovered my two great mentors, first my father and then my father-in-law, **Bob Galvin**. He used to say to his children, his in-laws, and his grandchildren that everything revolves around **trust**. Bob was the only son of Paul Galvin, the founder of a technology innovation company that he ultimately named Motorola. When Bob was seventeen, due to an unfortunate family situation, he came to work with his father at the Galvin Manufacturing Company. While he graduated from the University of Notre Dame, by that point his future was pretty well set, because his career with his father's company was gaining speed.

In 1959, at the age of thirty-seven, he succeeded his father as the CEO of the Motorola Corporation. His twenty-seven years in the CEO role as well as those in the subsequent chair's role brought great advances in technology and consumer products. As he always said, however, none of them would have happened had his father not trusted him. And on that basis, he built the business that grew to manufacture such cutting-edge technologies as the radio equipment on the early NASA space flights and the ubiquitous cellular telephone.

At one point in the history of Motorola, when sales were difficult, one of the senior leaders said at a meeting that "our quality sucks." Bob stopped the meeting, opted to pivot to that exact topic, and for the next years focused on building and selling quality products and services to its customers. Sometimes we are too close to it to see where the gaps lie, and we need one of our team members to tell us—we just need to listen. Bob was a fine mentor, but he was also an excellent listener.

I met my wife in 1985. That was pretty much when my father's career started to taper off, and that's when I met Bob Galvin. Bob was a very different kind of guy from my dad. He was much more stoic. He was much more introspective. Much more worldly in so many aspects. I started to sit with my father-in-law and really came to know him, and I also got an education in how big global companies really function. Bob had very, very high values and principles—he was an exceptionally ethical guy. He always felt that to be successful, any company or organization has to be built upon four equally powerful legs—creativity, leadership, ethics, and quality. He worked hard on establishing those four pieces of his business, and it was something he was always working on. He'd think hard about where the business could go and what it would look like down the road. My wife and her siblings have always said that their father was like chess master Bobby Fischer, in that he could always see six or seven moves ahead of what was happening in the moment. He was running a huge company in the present but always trying to build a company for the future.

For all his vision and success, it was also important to him to make sure everybody who was a part of the company's success got the recognition they deserved. He wanted to be considered not as the big boss but as just one more member of the team. To make that clear, he would wear a pocket protector with his name tag above it, and the tag simply said "Bob."

The stories of Bob's success and his teachings are legendary, but when I entered his life in 1985, due to falling in love with his oldest daughter, he always had time to talk with me and share his thoughts. In his mentoring role, some of the lessons he imparted on me were:

*"When you are looking for something, don't wait for it to come to you."*

Get in motion, and stay in motion, for motion's sake. Basically, you need to go out and find what you are looking for. The power of this advice first came to me when I was looking for a job. I needed to get out and scramble to find the right fit. To do so, I found myself scheduling meetings for breakfast, for coffee, for lunch, for drinks, for dinner—five a day. Invariably, if someone had nothing for me in their company, they would recommend two others I should speak to. My list got longer and longer! Five meetings a day was not enough. The job search revealed some thirty-seven different opportunities, which ran the gamut from president of an apparel company in New York, to owning a beer distributorship in Chicago, to president of Porsche Design, an international accessory company in Los Angeles, a company I ultimately joined.

*"Listen, listen, listen."*

As Bob and I would talk and he would ask me about my company or my business school, he would wait to impart any thoughts until I was asking him for his opinion. At that point, he would proffer a thought, fully vetted and defensible from so many angles. At his company, he would go to lunch in the employee cafeteria, come off the line with his tray, and look for where the engineers were. He'd go sit down with the engineers and say, "OK, guys, what are you working on? Tell me how it's going," and he would just listen. He was a great listener. And I learned a great lesson here about listening and learning. I had been told by a professor many years before, the hardest thing any leader can do is listen and learn. Bob was always ready to learn.

**You never know where/when you will find a mentor—keep your eyes open.**

As a dean of students, I tried to resist taking the role of family counselor. I was quite happy to counsel current and prospective students, but I felt that their choice of school or course of study was perhaps one of the first significant life choices they would be making as young adults, and they had the greatest chance of achieving success and happiness if they made those choices as independently as they could—free from the pressures of what their parents wanted for them. This led to some awkward family moments in my office, but I really wanted the decisions to be made by the students. I believed there was room for "bad" decisions, because in this case, they could be fixed. Majors could be switched; schools could be transferred in and out of. But I wanted these young adults to be making their own decisions—with their family's support.

**Questions About Your Family:**

- How do you think your appreciation of different family members has changed or will change through different stages of life and career?
- Do you have a friend who has had great relationships with their family members? What are the characteristics of those relationships that might be applicable to you?
- Is there anyone in your family who could be a mentor to you?

# CHAPTER 2

# Finding Your Wave

BACK IN 1986, I WAS IN THE MIDDLE OF A SIGNIFICANT CAREER shift. With fifteen years of management experience at The Broadway and Miller's Outpost behind me, I had launched my career as an entrepreneur, buying a small company in San Diego that distributed apparel such as Haggar slacks and Jockey underwear to military bases. The shift was not going all that well.

I was intrigued by the opportunity to build up a small company in an interesting niche market, and the fact that the company also did some product distribution to golf shops really appealed to me. My philosophy as a first-time business owner was that I wanted to make the company I bought not just a better place for clients—I also wanted to make it a better place for the people who worked there. I had learned through all those years in management that you can't get a company to work at its best unless you have the best people working there. I knew that your employees are your greatest asset in turning things around when there is a problem, and those employees usually know before anybody else what the problems are. My philosophy was not altruistic. I really did want people to be happy and satisfied working at my company, but I also believed that such happiness would translate into better service, happier clients, and a better bottom line. If my new career path was going to involve buying and selling companies, I definitely wanted to make money, but I also wanted to leave each company a better place than when I found it.

At the company in San Diego, there were some great people, and we had some exponential growth for a while. One of our successes was that we became one of the very first companies to supply apparel to the Price Club—the Southern California precursor to Costco. But the deal I cut with the owner I had bought the company from turned out to be messier than I imagined it would be. His continuing involvement in the company turned the experience sour for me. We got crossways on so many issues that I decided to sell the company back to him, and that transaction became even more of a hell to go through.

Finally, when the dust cleared, I could indeed consider myself an entrepreneur. I could also consider myself unemployed.

Back then, at the cusp of turning forty, I was also still single. I don't really remember exactly what I thought about the prospects of my love life at that point, but I'm pretty sure that if I had been asked what kind of woman I might fall in love with, I would have had some basic requirements: She would live in the same city I did; she would not have been married before; and she would not have children. As I have mentioned before, I did not expect the earth to move when an old friend of mine—a golf teammate from high school and college—suggested I go out on a blind date with a woman he thought I'd get along with—a divorcee with four children.

And who lived in Chicago. Chicago? I had trouble making a relationship work with someone from the other side of San Diego. And I realized that at this particular moment in my career, I might not look like much of a catch either. A clear-eyed look at the risk/benefit assessment should have told both of us to run away from each other, but our first date—in Chicago—went quite well. Well enough, in fact, that our second date was a week of skiing together in Vail. And at the end of that week, I asked her to marry me!!!

I hadn't met her family. I hadn't met her kids. We didn't know what city we were going to live in, and I wasn't sure where my next paycheck was going to come from. But, forty years later, Gail is still the love of my life, and our five children are a continual source of joy.

I bring this up not just to tell you how lucky I am to have the wife and family that I have, but also to introduce the concept of passion and how it can shape our lives and careers.

I think for most people, the most familiar form of passion is romance. We understand that a powerful feeling, not based strictly on logic or rational judgment, can compel us to commit to something that will completely change our life. Often, "passion" and "love" are used interchangeably, and while I may not be enough of a poet to explain all the nuances between the two, I would say that love is something with many varieties, while passion is a form of love that stems from absolute commitment of heart and soul. Logistics were not in favor of Gail and me getting together, but passion made all the difference. Once we were passionate about being together and making it work, all the big difficulties that might have derailed any other relationship became little challenges to be handled or worked around.

There are thousands of songs that celebrate the moment of falling in love, and we all pretty much know what the singer is singing about. But how do you find the equivalent passion in your career and your professional life?

In my years at USC as a teacher and as a dean, I was often in the position of offering career advice to students, and one of my common pieces of advice was for them to find something they were passionate about, because if they had a career that they were passionate about, it wouldn't feel like work. I stand by that advice, but I know it's not easy to put it into practice. Passion can be a hard thing for a college student to find. At a time in their lives when they can be overwhelmed by feelings of pressure, confusion, anxiety, and perhaps even general excitement for the adult life that awaits them, it can be very hard to identify an enduring passion that will see them through the challenges ahead and help clarify the choices they make. But I'd point out that the key word when we talk about passion is "find." You find your passion; you don't design it or make it happen according to a school schedule or work calendar. It can't be forced. You have to try to find it internally, as opposed to having someone else tell you that you will be great at a particular pursuit. Passion can't be replaced by encouragement—that is other people's passion on your behalf. The key here: Allowing yourself to remain open to the possibility of passion is the first step in finding it.

What if you don't find it? Is your career a nonstarter? Absolutely not. Things like hard work, responsibility, decency, common sense, and plain old luck are just as important to a successful career. You can work hard and do a competent job without being particularly passionate about it. And if you're overcome with passion but don't put in the hard work required to move yourself forward, the passion doesn't count for much. But all things being equal, passion becomes the great differentiator. It's what separates a great student from a good student, a great employee from a good employee, a great board member from a good board member, a great CEO from a good CEO. If you exude passion, everybody sees it in you. They see you have better drive and focus and commitment than someone else in the same discipline. It's truly the secret ingredient that pulls the whole recipe together.

In my professional life, the passion came as a surprise. I thought I was passionate about my work in management and passionate about my role as the CEO of a company. It turned out that I didn't understand what professional passion was until I stepped into the classrooms at USC and began teaching. The act of imparting knowledge to a new generation of eager minds fired up a passion in me that was an entirely new experience. I had no grand goal of becoming a dean—I was simply ecstatic about my job during my ten years as a teacher. Then, when I did have the opportunity to become dean, the passion kicked into overdrive. As a teacher I had the ability to impact 150 or so students a semester. As a dean, I had the ability to impact six thousand students, not just in terms of their classroom experiences, but in the shaping of their lives and careers to follow. At that point I wasn't just passionate about my work—my work became a central passion of my life.

This kind of passion had some tangible effects on my approach to the workday. I didn't look at the clock in terms of what time I was getting up or how late I was working or what time I was coming home. The work became all-encompassing, and at the same time it became satisfying in a way I hadn't felt before. I realized that in all my past positions, I had been conscientious, I had done a good job, and I had enjoyed the work. In fact, I don't think I ever did any job in my career that I didn't enjoy—and getting to the point where you can say that is not a bad goal. But the dean's job is the one I was truly passionate about. And that passion elevated me, and ultimately the school, to greater successes than I could have ever imagined.

Passion may not guarantee success. However, it will carry you through failure, and anyone engaged in the risks of a business career is sure to encounter a failure or two. The thing to keep in mind is that your passion will always put you one level above someone who is simply competent at their job—and is what makes your job feel exceptional to you. That's something worth finding.

I was hired as a professor at USC in 1997, but my first experience as a classroom teacher was actually back in the 1970s, when I taught a night class in marketing. I thought that, at the very least, having a class to show up for a couple of nights a week would keep me out of trouble. One of my students at the time was **Bob McKnight**. Bob came to me toward the end of the semester, to tell me he was graduating and was starting to think hard about what kind of job he might take to launch his career. When we met, we had an enjoyable, freewheeling discussion and came up with a lot options, but no concrete plan. We shared a good laugh when Bob concluded with an interesting metric for measuring what he hoped to accomplish—he told me that someday he would be successful and that I would work for him!

Bob was hugely passionate about the sport of surfing, and he decided he was going to treat himself to one last epic surfing adventure before starting a proper business career. He wanted to spend the summer riding the big waves in Australia and said he would come in to see me when he returned. In the fall, he did just that. He told me while in Australia, he'd met a man who made and sold a unique style of swim trunks that were becoming very popular with surfers Down Under. The trunks were made of a quick-drying fabric that was ideal for going in and out of the water. Perhaps drawing on skills he had honed in the marketing night class, Bob entered into some informal negotiations with the man and came back to the States a de facto licensee—with an agreement that he could make and sell the same swim trunks in the United States.

Bob knew how to look good in those shorts while surfing, but he had a lot of questions about setting up a business. Where would he buy the fabric he needed, how would he get the trunks designed and manufactured, and how would he price them and sell them? We talked through some business basics and the opportunities that might open up for him, and when he left that meeting, I had no doubt that he was eager to make this idea a reality.

Bob backed up his passion with a strong sense of principles in terms of how he wanted to run his business. He had great mentors to help him out, and he listened to them. When he began his business, he wanted to stay loyal to the surf shops along the California coast, and he preferred Quiksilver goods to be sold exclusively by them rather than in department stores or any chains of specialty stores. He wanted to establish a bond with his customers—his fellow surfers—so he designed his distribution strategy and stayed with it, even as huge sales opportunities opened up with other outlets. We argued about this numerous times, as by then I was deep into my retail career, but he would not deviate, and I came to respect his point of view. Once you know what you want and it is working, stay the course. Jumping from one lily pad to another doesn't always benefit the frog, and Bob proved that watery adage in his own way—riding out the wave he chose to surf.

Bob McKnight could have been a success doing something he wasn't passionate about—he's that talented at business. Instead, he created the perfect wave for himself, on which his passion and his work came together in an ideal way.

It would be hard to find an individual more passionate about what they do, and about life in general, than football coach **Pete Carroll**, who became head football coach at USC in late 2000.

Pete came to USC when the football program was in search of a new coach with winning ways, and he was definitely not considered a first choice. He'd had two stints as a head coach in the NFL, with the New York Jets and the New England Patriots, and neither had resulted in much success—in both cases he'd been fired after one or two seasons. But Pete was enthusiastic and persistent about winning the USC job. When he learned that one of the decision-makers involved had opted not to vote in his favor, he just kept pushing with others to get the job. I remember walking to my car one night and meeting the president of the university in the parking lot. He told me what was happening with the coach-hiring process and asked me what I thought about Pete's persistence. My response was that the situation was pretty easy to read—all things being equal, you hire the one who wants the job the most. He nodded, said thanks, and kept walking. Apparently, a majority of decision-makers felt the way I did because not long after Pete was hired.

Pete was the head coach at USC for nine years, and what he did for the football program has been well documented. Pete knew what had to be done to turn things around, and he knew how to make that happen. His mantra of "Win Forever" carried through everything that he, his coaches, and his players did. Losing was just not in the team's vocabulary as far as any of them were concerned. They worked hard to improve, and to be the best, but they knew that it was their intensity and passion that would carry the day.

Of particular importance to me in my relationship with Pete was his attitude of always helping where he could. If we were trying to convince a great student to matriculate to USC, and we needed to get them across the finish line, Pete was always willing to talk to them. If we needed to motivate our students in a class, Pete was there to speak to the class. If I needed a commencement speaker, Pete was always ready and willing to do the job, his schedule permitting. That "team spirit" worked both ways—if Pete needed to pitch an athlete on coming to the school, he was never shy about asking me to help the pitch.

When Pete left USC to become head coach of the Seattle Seahawks, I felt bad for us, but great for him. It meant he felt confident enough to go back to a place where he had had little success, and make it happen.

Even as he achieved phenomenal success in Seattle, Pete never forgot us. He and the sports psychologist Michael Gervais worked with our USC entrepreneurship people to start the Peak Performance Institute: a center designed to help business executives be at the top of their game when it was most needed. They came to campus to talk to students and collaborated with our team to develop curricula and helped raise the funds to make it sustainable. It is a true area of development for business education—we know how to excel at numbers, but how do we keep our head in the game when faced with challenges and obstacles? Pete has put just as much passion into developing this business program as he puts into his game plans.

When he left the Seahawks, Pete agreed to teach a class at USC, again with the passion that made him successful, and the students signed up in droves. And, as I write this, he has left the job as the head coach of the Las Vegas Raiders—the naysayers think he is too old at seventy-three. They don't know Pete like I know Pete—I will never bet against him, ever.

If I learned one thing from Pete Carroll, it's that "Win Forever" isn't just a football cheer. It's a philosophy for life that reminds one to be focused and persistent in achieving one's goals. Adopting a "Win Forever" philosophy doesn't mean there won't be some losses on your record—there will be. But passion for winning will ultimately make you a winner.

Student passions can be infectious but can also be mercurial. The lives of young people can be in such a state of flux that passions can flare up and flame out very quickly. It's always a challenge to figure out what passions may be short-lived and which one may be life shaping, but it would always be a mistake to write off youthful passion as simple idealism.

One of the benefits of having great students at USC was the chance to meet some great parents. One such parent was **Julia Stewart**. At the age of sixteen, Julia went to work as a waitress at the International House of Pancakes (IHOP). Something about the bustle of a well-run kitchen and the smiles of satisfied customers resonated deeply with her. At that young age, in a job many might consider a short-term venture, she found her passion and her career path. She earned a degree in communications but remained powerfully drawn to the food service industry. From dealing with the early challenges of delivering plates of short stacks and Belgian waffles to hungry tables, Julia worked her way up to become president of IHOP's sister company, Applebee's, then became chair and CEO of IHOP, then rose to CEO of Dine Equity, the $11 billion parent company of IHOP and Applebee's.

As a young waitress, Julia quickly understood how important the customer is to any business, and as her job responsibilities grew, she never forgot that lesson. Her passion for customer service, quality of product, and cleanliness of venue became guiding principles in the hundreds of restaurants she oversaw.

As the end of one school year approached, I was looking for a female CEO to address the Marshall graduates at their commencement ceremony. It occurred to me that Julia would be an excellent choice, and I was thrilled when she accepted the role. She was a wonderfully engaging speaker and spoke to the grads extensively about another quality they needed to possess—courage.

Julia still brings passion to everything she does, and her own courage has pushed her to take on new challenges. Today, she is the CEO of a start-up, Alurx, that allows her to combine her passion for serving the consumer with her skills as a leader and teacher. The new company is in the health and wellness space and offers products and services to consumers that will help them on their journey to good health. Julia has thought through every detail—from the messages of the product packaging to the tone of the company's marketing materials—and her passion for the betterment of her customers couldn't be clearer. In the cutthroat business worlds of restaurants and online retail, profit margins can be slim, failure rates high, and success elusive. Julia Stewart is a great example of how when facing such challenges, courage and personal passion can make all the difference.

Today, **Kevin Kassel** is the CEO and founder of Aqus LLC—which he started when he was in his undergraduate years. He won a number of awards for his business idea and plan, and he promptly set out to change the world.

Kevin's idea (and his passion) was to solve the global water crisis by designing water filters that would be affordable to the people who need them the most. Aqus designs, manufactures, and sells the only affordable, income-generating water filters created specifically for consumers in the developing world. These filters eliminate the need to purchase bottled water or to boil contaminated water, and they provide a more affordable, safer, and environmentally friendly alternative. For poorer consumers, Aqusafe water filters have the capability to filter enough water daily to allow them to become water entrepreneurs, generating a supplemental income by selling water to people in their communities.

Kevin had the intelligence and the business sense to make his idea work—he never stopped networking and asking for help. It has been his passion for making a difference in the lives of others that has been the true engineer of his success.

Another success story from my marketing class was actually a finance major—**Brandon Beck**—who was just a great student, regardless of the topic at hand. He graduated and went to work in the consulting business. That, however, was not his passion—he loved to play video games.

He called one of his fellow USC classmates, Mark Merrill, and suggested they design a game together. In 2006, they turned their passion for enjoyment into of the most successful companies of its time, Riot Games, which produced one of the most-played games of all time, the League of Legends. Their concept for this game was different from what other companies in the space were offering. With League of Legends, you could download the game for free, but to truly win big you needed to buy some weapons. This was a new twist on the razor-and-blades concept pioneered by Gillette—a highly successful marketing strategy.

When they sold half of Riot Games to a Chinese firm, they really had reached the pinnacle of success, but to their credit, they never changed. They stayed to run the company and continue to grow it—always loyal to the gamers they served. They were passionate about their company and their customers, and they ultimately became great philanthropists as well.

Another student who is truly passionate about her path in life is one I met in the classroom as an undergraduate. **Devita Saraf** showed leadership from the start with her preparedness, her participation, and her after-class discussions with me. She wanted to be not just a success, but a leader of women in her home country of India, and to show them by example how it could be done.

Straight out of college she developed a business plan and assembled a core team around her. Her interest in cutting-edge technology led her to found Vu Televisions—a brand of high-definition smart TVs that were designed to have particular appeal to millennials, offering up such features as built-in entertainment-based apps and built-in computer operating systems. Marketing a game-changing, new style of a familiar product meant that sales were slow at first, but Devita wisely took a "long game" approach to developing her company—more interested in running a marathon than a sprint. She also took the bold step of being a face-forward CEO, making herself an often-seen and very approachable representative of her brand in a country where female executives are often not taken as seriously as male counterparts.

Now twenty years after her graduation, Devita is the CEO of the Vu Group, a technology conglomerate that has expanded into lifestyle, workstyle, and communications brands. Despite the expansion, Devita has kept her company lean and nimble enough that during the pandemic of 2020, she was one of the few executives who did not have to fire any employees or cut any salaries. In fact, at a time when more people were watching more TV, she seriously expanded the customer service element of her company.

Devita has been named one of the Best 40 under 40 leaders in India—and, given the number of successful young entrepreneurs there, that is saying something. Staying true to her original passion for inspiring others, Devita leads by example—she is a hands-on mentor who has given over 150 talks to groups of young women about turning their dreams into reality.

One of the true pleasures of my job over the years has been the chance I've had to counsel high school students on their college decisions—where to matriculate and how to get there. In that role, I met with the son of **Steve Ballmer**, who was then still the CEO of Microsoft. Steve's son, Sam, was a calm, centered high school student who listened carefully to what I had to say about USC and eventually became a very successful student there. In the course of that counseling, I also got to meet Steve himself and frankly, "calm and centered" is not the phrase that comes to mind when describing him. Meeting with Steve is like meeting with a friendly hurricane—the passion he has for his family, his business, for everything he does is barely containable.

The first hint I had of Steve's passionate nature was when I learned he had spent a day wandering around the USC campus incognito to get an unbiased feel for the school his son might be attending. And whatever his own impressions of the school were, his love for his son was such that when it came time to make a decision, Steve simply asked his son, "Is this where you want to be?" and accepted the "Yes" he got as an answer.

With his son enrolled and making steady progress toward a degree, I was a little surprised when Steve called a couple of years later and requested a ninety-minute meeting with me. My assistant was quick to point out to him that I never seemed to be able to sit through any meeting that long, but Steve persisted. He was transitioning out of his position at Microsoft and wanted some intensive, one-on-one career counseling. He was looking for objectivity and a supportive sounding board with which to explore the many options open to him. That's just what he did—we spent an exciting hour and a half together talking about the various "second acts" he might pursue in his professional life. It was a very spirited, unrestrained meeting, and every time Steve began to explain one of his ideas, the explanation itself seemed to spark a whole new set of ideas that needed to be thought through. Steve's intelligence and passion were on full display. At the end of the ninety minutes, we had not resolved anything for him, but he seemed even more passionate about his future than he had when the meeting began. It really struck me that a man of such confidence—a man who had already achieved such success—also had the humility to ask someone else for frank advice. The agenda for our discussion was Steve and his future, and that's what we stuck to, but he wanted to be questioned and challenged. Being passionate doesn't mean you are so ego driven that you can't hear what others are saying, and that you are never above asking for opinions of others.

Steve did go on to pursue some personal passions in a big way. He bought the Los Angeles Clippers basketball team—a dream come true for him. And he established both his family's philanthropic foundation, the Ballmer Group, which supports efforts to improve economic mobility for those living in poverty, and USAFacts.org, a nonprofit organization whose goal is to allow people to understand government revenue, spending, and societal impact. Steve may have made history—and his fortune—with Microsoft, but his passion continues to drive him to have a positive societal impact in hugely meaningful ways. Most recently, he and his wife Connie agreed to match funds raised in a concert to help the wildfire victims of the Southern California wildfires of 2025, and that will have a huge impact on many lives of those who lost homes or were displaced.

Someone who has become a close friend and whose passion I have admired from close up is **Margaret Spellings**, who has served as the United States secretary of education, as the CEO of the George W. Bush Library in Dallas, and as the president of the University of North Carolina's seventeen-campus system.

Those of us who go into academia are making a clear career choice, and more often than not that choice has to be driven by a passion for education; if one is mainly concerned with the accumulation of wealth, there are certainly more lucrative fields of pursuit in the private sector. Margaret started her career in the political arena but always seemed to display an interest in education issues. She felt that the political structure of the country had to be aligned to bring the best education to its young people and worked hard to do that. Convening the Spellings Commission while a cabinet secretary, she worked to ensure that higher education could effectively prepare graduates for their move into the workplace. She had helped the "No Child Left Behind" initiative for President George W. Bush and wanted to be sure that initiative was carried through postsecondary education.

Having worked at the national level in education, she moved to a university presidency, hoping to bring a positive change at that level. In both areas, she had to put aside notions of personal gain and keep her passions focused on how to improve the larger systems. It was difficult to operate within the bureaucracies of national government– and university-level academics, but she wanted badly to have an impact that would make things better for so many young people. At the university, passions could not quite carry her past bureaucracy, and after a few years of service, she reluctantly resigned. Her passion for education has never faded, though, and is still the driving force behind her professional endeavors. She now heads up the Bipartisan Policy Center in Washington, DC, working to craft viable solutions that improve lives, as it says on its website—she will make that happen.

There will be a lot of situations in a professional career in which outcomes cannot be controlled, and sometimes having passion for what you do does not mean you'll be able to control outcomes any better than others. But passion does have a value—it doesn't dictate the outcome, but it does make a difference in the mindset one adopts when trying to achieve a desired outcome. Passion is also cumulative—it builds up over time. You don't know if or when the reward is going to come, but passion will always push you toward success.

No one loves a new idea more than **Tim Draper**. One of the most successful venture capital investors in Silicon Valley, Tim has learned there are no bad ideas, just some that need a little tweaking to make them better.

Having founded a venture capital firm with two partners in the mid-eighties, Tim hit on a winner in Hotmail, quickly followed by Baidu—he was one of the earliest investors to see value in a Chinese start-up. His list of larger successes includes Skype and Tesla. At the beginning of the cryptocurrency craze, Tim led the charge into bitcoin, proclaiming it to be heading toward huge multiples down the road. His absolute passion for big ideas is something that sometimes leads him astray, but he does not have a problem accepting strikeouts along with home runs. He knows that a balance of hits and misses is all part of the game he loves.

Tim's passion has brought Draper University of Heroes to the world, a training ground for young entrepreneurs. My youngest son attended the school and felt so moved by Tim's approach that he still says, "I would do anything for Tim Draper." Tim had a similarly inspiring effect when he came to USC to give the commencement address to the business undergrads. He talked about maintaining a passion for what you're doing, and how you keep moving forward. Don't give up just because you hit a pothole in the road. The students knew they were listening to a successful, battle-scarred veteran of many investment skirmishes and were deeply impressed by his passionate and creative mind.

As passionate as Tim is, his investment decisions are never made without strong empirical analysis first—the market, the competition, and the timing. Sometimes, luck is involved as well, but good decision-making tools need to be included in the process.

Still, some of his slips have been notable. One year he suggested that California should be broken up into six states and had some great logic and statistics to back him up. He was almost able to get that initiative on the state ballot that year, but the passion he felt for this idea wasn't shared by many others. He also backed the failed start-up Theranos, having first met its founder, Elizabeth Holmes, when she was a young family friend. But those types of misses do not deter him from getting up and going again, and he learns from each mistake.

One of the most passionate people who has come through my life is a former student, **Sourena Vasseghi**. His passion has manifested itself in so many ways, as he has journeyed a difficult path in life.

Sourena was born with the umbilical cord wrapped around his neck, and his doctors quickly assumed that he had passed away in childbirth and set the infant aside so they could pay attention to his mother. As he lay on the table, given up for dead, Sourena started to cry—scaring the doctors and launching them into action. He was alive and needed immediate attention. The result of that difficult birth was that Sourena contracted cerebral palsy and has used a wheelchair since childhood. He has very little control over the physical movements of his body, and his speech is barely understandable. What is very obvious is the brain power that is inside his head, his passionate desire to be taught and to learn, and to succeed.

As a graduating high school student, Sourena decided that he wanted to attend the University of Southern California, and he went to a community college so he could achieve the grades he needed to transfer. He knew it would be an uphill climb, but then again, when had his life not been? He transferred, and that is where I came to know him—he took three classes from me during his undergraduate years.

My classes were mostly taught with the Socratic case method, where students needed to participate in class, contributing to the discussion and helping to come to a solution for the problem being examined. Sourena's hand was always in the air. Many times, I could not understand what he was saying, but his classmates were great at translating for me. He was always on point and had very insightful questions that seemed to indicate a much wider range of work experience than he'd actually had. Students would ask me after class, "If Sourena has never been on a shop floor or in an office, how does he even know how to ask the questions he asks?"

During his time at USC, he and I spent many hours together, discussing his future. It was hard, as he knew that companies would have difficulty hiring him—they would not know where he could serve them best. He wanted to be financially independent, to have a family, and to live the closest thing to a "normal" life that he could have. Ultimately, I suggested to him that to achieve these goals, maybe he should write a book, and then go out on a speaking tour. Why struggle to be hired by an entrepreneur when he could be one himself? Of course, as one might imagine, his comeback was, "I can't write, and I can't speak." True, true.

A young man, Jay Lavender, whose parents had introduced me to my wife, was an up-and-coming screenwriter in Hollywood. He had grown up with a friend who had cerebral palsy, and he could understand what Sourena said. He agreed to talk with him and possibly help him write the book. Soon thereafter, the book was finished: *Love Your Life and It Will Love You Back.* Sourena self-published it, and in its first three weeks on Amazon, it was a bestseller!

With huge passion for what he was doing, Sourena hired people to help him speak—acting as translators for his words. They prepared talks for high school students, for Rotary and Kiwanis clubs, and even for college students. He practiced and was able to insert jokes into the talks as well. It was tough sledding at first, but there were great rewards in what Sourena's passion had led him to accomplish.

Then, Sourena's life did indeed love him back. One morning, Jay, the writer, called my office—he demanded that I be interrupted in my meeting and stayed on the line until I picked up. He asked if I had spoken with Sourena that day, and I told him I had not. He said that he would get him on the line, which he did, and told Sourena to tell me what happened. It took two times for him to say it, such that I understood: His mother had won the lottery! She and an office colleague had split a lottery ticket and had all the winning numbers. She was a bookkeeper and her husband had owned a pizza shop, but with her half of the winnings, her family was set for life and could provide a better life for Sourena and his sister. If anyone deserved it, this family did. I could not have been more excited for them.

I spoke with the family at length about how to pay any debts they had, how to find the right financial advisors, and how to protect their winnings. I wanted to be sure that the family could sustain themselves and spend their new money wisely. Sourena now has the financial ability to pursue his passion—his book and his speaking engagements—and he wanted to add executive coaching and other initiatives to his portfolio. He could test different directions to go, and even fail if they were wrong. It was lifting a huge weight off everyone's shoulders.

The money did not deter Sourena from his studies. He earned his degree and was very excited to take part in the graduation ceremony. I used to tell my students that when their name was called at graduation, they would walk across the stage to get their diploma but walk very slowly. This is your hard-earned first fifteen seconds of fame—give your parents a gift and take it slow. On Sourena's graduation day, he was up on the stage in his wheelchair when they called his name—the last of the ceremony. He got a bit overexcited and started having a hard time controlling his movements. He could barely grab the joystick on his chair, and when he finally hit it, he just about popped a wheelie. The chair flew across the stage and screeched to a halt right before he got to the dean. The dean put the diploma in his lap and Sourena turned around, just about popped a wheelie again, and flew back across the stage. What he didn't see was that his entire class was giving him a standing ovation. He sent me an email that night in regard to my advice about moving slowly. "Dear Jim, I screwed up. I went too fast."

After graduating, Sourena came back to campus often to speak to students. During one of these visits, he told me that he had fallen in love and was about to marry a young woman. The next year, he told me that his wife was pregnant! He was off to the races, living out his dreams and passions. Sourena's passion is what keeps his mind so active in all regards.

He is always thinking about what is around the next turn in the road, and how he might make whatever he discovers work to his advantage, even given his physical infirmities. He's had plenty of reasons to surrender to the difficulties of his life, but he refuses to accept that mindset.

**Love your life and it will love you back!**

**Questions About Your Own Passions:**

- Have you ever been passionate about a job you held?
- If someone were to ask you today to look at the next twenty-five years of your life as a clean sheet of paper, meaning you could fill that blank page with anything you were passionate about, what would that paper look like?
- What career would allow you to pursue one of your passions?
- What are ALL the many careers that you could pursue that would help you follow your passions?

Same guy—just what seventy-five years of experience looks like.

My parents' college graduation.

Mom and Dad—my first mentors—even if they didn't know it.

Brother Mark, sister Chris.

Mom, Dad, sister Chris, brother Mark—family support is so meaningful.

Our wedding day, March 22, 1987—best day of my life.

Mom Mary, brothers Mike and Chris, sister Dawn—more family support.

Gail's dad, Bob Galvin.

With Gail's mom Mary and dad Bob—such great supporters of us both.

Our entire nuclear family—us with kids and grandkids.

Happiness at Tiffany's wedding in Vail on New Year's Eve.

Our Saturday morning coffee group—over twenty-five years of friendship together.

## Chapter 3

# The Bill Gates Conundrum

### *Is Business Education Worth It?*

There are two types of education, formal and informal, and both serve purposes. In school, where you are formally educated, you learn the skill sets you will need to get you through your careers, whatever those turn out to be. Informal education gives you separate skill sets to get through life, which will equip you to handle the twists and turns that come your way (and they will come).

It is so interesting to me that we remember our BEST teachers in school, and we remember our WORST teachers. That doesn't count for most of our teachers; the vast remainder who don't rank among the best and worst are long forgotten. I would contend that those teachers in the forgotten middle had an influence on us as well, but just not as strongly or memorably as the best and worst did. The ability to teach is a talent that comes about from someone who truly cares about what they are doing—it can't be fully developed by someone who is just going through the motions in a classroom in order to collect a paycheck. Good teachers don't teach to be remembered—they teach because they care about what they are doing, and care about how we respond to their talents.

When it comes to our informal educations, something similar holds true: We can remember great pieces of advice we received, and some terrible pieces of advice we received, but sometimes it is hard to assess just how much the people around us have taught us. We leave each job, we become a little wiser and more experienced, and every relationship we have influences who we are as a person, but it's hard to be aware of all of our growth as it is happening. Likewise, you might not see that day-to-day growth of a tree—but you become aware that what was once an acorn is now a mighty oak.

The role of education has been important in my life, and that of my family's. It was never up for debate in my home whether my siblings and I would attend college—you just knew that you would be finished with your education after sixteen years, not the basic twelve. Paying the tuition, while always an issue involving some sacrifice, was something that my parents assumed they would figure out how to manage, and they made it happen for all of us. Today, the value of a college degree has increased, while the cost of tuition has skyrocketed. Families that want to send their children to college can be faced with some extremely difficult financial situations.

Adding up my time in grade school, high school, college, and business school, I went through eighteen straight years of education (actually seventeen, as I skipped the first grade!). Later, after Gail and I were married, all five of our kids earned college degrees, and two of them went on to earn advanced degrees as well. As in the homes Gail and I grew up in, in our home there was never much discussion about whether our kids would attend college—they went through the application process, headed off to their various campuses, pursued their studies of choice, and generally enjoyed the experience. As I have told many undergraduates, the college years are the time of your life when just about everyone wishes they were you—high school kids can't wait to leave home and get a taste of the freedom college affords, and those who are older pine for the school years that were so rich and open ended with possibility (not to mention the summer vacations and holiday breaks that are not standard issue in the working world). The college years are a time when you have no greater responsibility than to define yourself for yourself, and you are encouraged and even expected to have a great deal of fun while you learn.

I think it's very important to point out that those expectations—academic success while having "the best years of your life"—can be a stress-inducing burden. At college, for the first time in your life, you may be offered the chance to enjoy newfound freedom and responsibility, but those early steps into adult life can be accompanied by tremendous fears and anxiety. Much has been written about how today's college students are more anxious than ever, but anxiety is not a new problem. When I was at Harvard decades ago, I had the horrific experience of actually hearing the gunshot when a fellow student took his own life. He'd made it through the seven rounds of interviews with a potential employer but had been dropped before the eighth and final round. In the high-pressure cauldron of business school, he apparently couldn't imagine living beyond that perceived failure.

Colleges and universities have become much better at dealing with issues of stress and anxiety more proactively, and it is hard these days to find a school that doesn't offer a full range of mental health services. As a dean, I certainly dealt with a number of stressed-out students, and my advice was usually to encourage them to shift their perspective a bit. Instead of being overwhelmed by social media and academic expectations, turn those feelings around and try to take some pleasure in the challenge of discovering who you are. Think failure and rejection might be in your immediate future? Great! Dealing with those things is a skill everyone could use in life, and now you've got a head start in developing that skill. Maybe some of your classmates seem to achieve perfect emotional balance through a few rounds of beer pong. Fine. If learning to confront the world on your own feels like hard work, that's OK—because it is hard work, but it's hard work that will eventually pay off in wonderful ways.

At Marshall, I tried to keep in mind that I might be the first authority figure in a student's life who has ever treated them as a fellow adult. At the same time, if a student was thousands of miles from home for the first time in their life and feeling lost or confused about what classes to take or how to pay for the next semester, I was not just an authority figure but an extension of the family support system. Sometimes it was the student's family that needed more emotional support than the student. Boundaries had to be maintained—my job was to be everybody's dean, not everybody's uncle. But the goal for everyone was for the student to have a satisfying and successful educational experience, and it was always gratifying to see how many of these students responded to just a little bit of guidance and encouragement.

The pressure some students feel today is directly tied to the cost of higher education. Tuition and housing costs have put many colleges and universities out of the reach of too many students. In my years at USC, I did whatever I could to help raise money for scholarships, and we had some great results. My general feeling has always been that if a student graduates from high school and is accepted to a university, they have done what they were expected to do, and they deserve to go there. At the Marshall School of Business, when we found students who we felt would be a great addition to the school, we wanted to do what we could to help their families get those kids there. Not only did the kids receiving those scholarships benefit greatly, but the school itself became stronger (and higher ranked).

In my position at USC Marshall, I tried to make those paths accessible, and I was proud to be a part of charting a few new paths that hadn't existed before. Believing that exposure to travel is a fantastic method of education, the school developed a World Bachelor in Business program—in which undergraduates with an international bent studied at USC; at the Hong Kong University of Science and Technology; and at Bocconi University in Milan, Italy; and then received degrees from all three institutions. In addition, Marshall was also able to offer a Master of Business for Veterans, to teach those returning from conflicts around the world some of the basic tenets of business.

The more that institutions of higher education can offer divergent and creative paths to students, the greater will be their standing in the community and the successes of their students. In today's world, just offering an undergraduate degree is not enough—it needs to be one with accessibility, one with purpose, and one where students can see the opportunities for themselves down the road.

The lines between formal and informal education have begun to blur a bit. The popularity of the "gap year" in which a student defers their acceptance to a college or university is a great example. It allows a student essentially to make a year of life experience and informal education a part of the formal program. Part-time studies and night classes do the same thing—individuals lead their "real" lives while balancing that with formal education. I like this concept of blended education, because from my perspective, in a well-lived life, the schooling never stops. I was a college student, then a business school student. I learned to be a businessman working for others. Then I learned to be a boss. Then I learned to be an entrepreneur. Then I learned to be a teacher and finally, I learned how to be a dean. Along the way I learned to be a husband, a father, and a friend.

Yes, sorry to say that education is never really over—it remains critical to your success in life. The trick is simply to find joy in the fact that there is always more to know.

One of the great advocates for education has been my friend **Austin Beutner**. Austin stepped down in June 2021 after three grueling years as the superintendent of the Los Angeles Unified School District, the second-largest school district in the United States. He was there during the very difficult time of the pandemic, with a system in transition, and yet brought that system to a new level of functionality, with a stronger commitment to students' well-being. He established standards of excellence that will greatly influence the LA school district for years to come. Through a very challenging time, Austin took on issues not just of reading, writing, and arithmetic, but also food insecurity, housing insecurity, mental illness, the digital divide, and the procurement of resources for a chronically ill underfunded system.

If one were to trace through the career Austin has had—and it is not over yet, as he set his sights on the job of mayor of the city of Los Angeles!—it is hard to see how he would end up in the field of education. He followed a most imperfect path to a superintendent's job, and that in itself is a great lesson: If you build a strong foundation of expertise and remain open to new challenges, that expertise will turn out to be invaluable in some unexpected places.

After graduating from Dartmouth, Austin spent fourteen years in the financial services industry, first as a financial analyst with Smith Barney and then as a partner with the Blackstone Group. In 1996, he cofounded Evercore Partners, an investment banking advisory firm, which successfully went public ten years after its founding.

Austin developed a good base of understanding finance, and he recognized how important the numbers were to any organization. That knowledge and experience allowed him to make some significant jumps in his career. He followed his stint at Evercore with government work, as a member of the Clinton administration's State Department assigned with assisting post-Soviet Russia's shift from a communistic society to a free market economy. Then, he focused on more domestic concerns, serving as the deputy mayor of Los Angeles and working to make LA a more business-centered city. He went on to cochair a commission that examined the financial health of Los Angeles, aiming to make its city entities more customer oriented and environmentally aware. Austin's business mind was a singular, reliable asset as he continued to push himself out of his comfort zone.

During his time cochairing the commission, Austin and I worked together to bring a large Chinese manufacturing company to the Los Angeles area, competing with several other American cities that wanted the company to locate with them. Austin was an expert at bringing together community, proving that Angelenos can work together and make things happen when following effective leadership. The effort was a success, bringing jobs to the area and a great boost to the local economy.

Somehow, Austin's path led next to his being named publisher and CEO of the *Los Angeles Times*. Oh no, a businessman in a journalism world! Well, far from being just a bottom-line thinker, Austin led a surge in the popularity of the newspaper, fueled by his encouragement of reporters to dig for important stories, his push for expanded foreign coverage, his outreach to LA's ethnic communities, and his eye for the financial health of the paper.

During his thirteen-month tenure at the helm of the paper, the *Times* won a Pulitzer Prize and a number of national journalism awards. This was all done in an environment when newspaper readership was in steep decline.

Austin wasn't done challenging himself. He created a task force to look into issues of the Los Angeles Unified School District—a business mind in a significant sector other than business. That led directly to his selection as the superintendent of LAUSD. He worked hard in that role to give disadvantaged students access to materials that they might not otherwise have had. He worked hard to get kids to come to school. He worked hard to give them access from home to their learning objectives.

Successful careers are built by people who take risks, as Austin has; who work hard, as Austin has; and who cares, as Austin does. The students at the Los Angeles Unified School District saw him in their schools when they came in the morning, and they knew he was behind them all the way. He brought a wealth of knowledge gained in the business, government, and journalism sectors to the education sector, and while he has been subject to criticism and setbacks, every endeavor that he has been a part of has been improved by his involvement.

Some years ago, I received an email from a United States naval officer who was serving our country in a distant combat zone. He asked me if I might help him, as he was so far away and he needed to procure some financial assistance so that his newly admitted son could attend USC. It was very obvious that education was of utmost importance to the officer and his wife, as they wanted their children to have the best they could get, if they could figure out a way to deal with the price tag of a topflight education.

Continuing to communicate via email, the officer and I worked together, and our Financial Aid office was able to find scholarship monies so their son could attend the university of his choice. He did extremely well at USC and successfully graduated. This, however, is not the end of the story.

Through our interactions, I became friends with the officer, **Collin Green**, who is a retired three-star vice admiral in the United States Navy, and the former commander of the Naval

Special Warfare Command—we know them as the Navy SEALs. His attention to duty and service to his country is second only to his attention to the well-being of his family and his duties as a father of four children. We have had many discussions about the value of education—he himself is a graduate of the United States Naval Academy.

So, while he has spent many months of his long naval career away from home and family, protecting our country and the troops under his watch, he has always been very concerned with how his kids were doing in school back home, and with what kind of futures they were developing for themselves. I had the pleasure of seeing three of his four children matriculate through USC, and I can say from firsthand experience that they embody the spirit that their father has for learning.

He understands that knowledge is power, and that education is the best preparation for the rigors of battle, or the rigors of life. He is in a position to be a teacher to many, but he has never stopped being a student either and is always eager to learn. As the Green family has worked their way through USC, Collin and I have spoken many times about the importance of education in preparing for the next steps. Education is the basis for many successful lives, and whether on a battleship, on a campus, or in the boardroom, those who learn to be prepared for the unexpected always have an advantage over those who haven't done the prep work.

A great teacher in the classroom came from a most unusual job prior to becoming a professor—that of a naval aviator. **Captain Jack Dittrick** also graduated from the United States Naval Academy, and while flying jets, managed to get his master's and doctorate degrees. During his time at Annapolis, he had been the roommate of senator-to-be John McCain, to whom Jack may have roughed out a few lectures while developing his teaching skills.

Jack was calm but strong, kind but decisive, very funny, and above all, highly ethical. His naval career was marked with great successes. I only learned those successes later on, because it was as a professor and associate dean that I first came to know him.

When I first came to USC on a full-time basis in the late nineties, Jack asked me to serve on a board overseeing the undergraduate program. One might imagine that a teacher with a military background would bring a certain rigidity to the classroom, but watching Jack in action, I saw a tremendous innovator. Rather than simply dispense lectures leading up to an exam, Jack was always looking for new ways to challenge his students. He created a national competition for undergraduate students to showcase their talents, and in order to bring fresh energy and ideas to the USC campus, he traveled the world recruiting international standouts.

I learned a great deal about the art of conducting a meeting from **Renee Kauffman**. She was a facilitator/trainer for YPO who brought a most impressive resume to the job—three degrees from Northwestern University, as well as experience in her family's business. She had a demeanor of utmost confidence in what she advocated, which happened to be some very practical teachings.

Meetings are a necessary part of the business world, and also a part that almost everyone dreads. It has always been amazing to me how many ways meetings can go wrong. There are meeting leaders who let attendees ramble or take over the agenda, or they lose control completely and do not recognize that an agenda has turned to chaos until it is too late. Many come into the meeting without an agenda or an idea as to what they want to accomplish.

What I learned from Renee was that a few critical concepts have to be enforced for a meeting to be successful. She taught me that there should always be name cards at meetings, so everyone knows where to sit and to whom they're talking. In commenting on someone else's idea, one should never begin with, "You should . . ." but rather, "Have you ever thought about . . ." or, "Have you ever considered . . ." She said that when running a meeting, one should be firm about when the meeting starts and ends. If you tell your team that the meeting will be over at 2 p.m., then end it by 2 p.m., if not sooner—never later. Additionally, be sure to block times during the meeting that will help you get through the agenda, leaving room for questions/discussions, allowing you to finish on time. Additionally, being calm as a facilitator and knowing the sequence you use in bringing speakers into the discussion is important. Who should follow whom, with similar or differing views, is important to building a conversation, and that is a talent that good meeting leaders have. They can orchestrate the meeting if they know their attendees and their agendas.

Renee was never a professor, but if we had offered a "meeting" major at Marshall, she would have been an exceptional one. She was excellent in her role—no one better—and taught many of us "the art of the meeting."

A true entrepreneur and wonderful teacher of burgeoning entrepreneurs, **Tom O'Malia** led a group of people who developed the study of entrepreneurship in universities. Tom developed the course of study himself and was given full authority to establish his courses at USC. He instituted classes on feasibility, business plan development, and implementation—totally nonacademic by definition but extremely practical to those students wishing to start a business of their own. Coupled with the academic courses that students took, the combination of Tom's classes gave them a great start on careers as self-starters, and great insight into what they had to do to control their own destinies. The program was actually started prior to Tom's arrival on campus but grew significantly on his watch. Many successful businesses were spawned in his classrooms.

As a teacher, Tom was tough, thorough, and compassionate. He knew what it took to start something and make it happen. To that end, he finished every phone call and email with "Hey, go MAKE it a great day." He did not say "Have a great day," but rather suggested that you control the day and make it good. Regardless of how bleak things may look and how many speed bumps are put in your pathway, ultimately the most important decisions in your life are in your control.

An extremely successful global businessman came into my office one day and showed me how invaluable education is to good business. **Jorge Paulo Lemann** had a difficult start at Harvard but graduated nonetheless—and he parlayed that education into a great career.

First, however, he had a little competing to do in the athletic area. He won the Brazilian national tennis championship five times, and then competed on both Brazil and Swiss Davis Cup teams international events. And he played at Wimbledon. He turned his athletic skills into a great career, during which he learned a lot about how to compete and how to win.

As he built his business career, JP took lessons from every experience he had and built on them—he was very innovative in his approach to business. By the time I met him, he had cofounded 3G Capital, which he built into a megacompany that encompassed such interests as Heinz, Kraft, Anheuser-Busch, and Burger King. He and his team worked hard to take excess expenses out of those companies, making them leaner and meaner.

But the day he walked into my office, it was not to talk about acquisitions and operating companies, but rather the education of students from Brazil. He was concerned about kids in his home country and wanted us to help them learn about entrepreneurship. He felt that Americans made the best entrepreneurs, and he wanted those in his country to learn from the best. USC has since graduated about ten master's students in entrepreneurship and innovation from Brazil, with more coming through.

Those of us who have been in academia still see tremendous value in undergrad and graduate degrees, but we have to contend with some "legends" of the business world. Today's would-be students can point to the likes of Bill Gates, Steve Jobs, or Mark Zuckerberg—none of whom completed even their undergraduate degrees—and ask, "If I've got a great idea, why not skip school and start my own company?" Well, that approach certainly worked for those three, but there are thousands of failed start-ups that would attest to the riskiness of such an approach. I would argue that the business world still puts a premium on an individual's credentials, so why not arm yourself with the credentials of a BA and/or an MBA? Those degrees will point you in the direction of success and will also give you some crucial room to fail. If a business idea or a start-up doesn't work out, those degrees still give you value, particularly if you have to restart.

If degrees are to be pursued, then students interested in business careers face an early major decision at the undergraduate level: If they intend to pursue a business-oriented degree at the graduate level, what is the appropriate undergraduate major? For many years, educators felt that everything a student might need to know about the business world would be taught at the graduate level. The thoughts as to which undergraduate major would best prepare for grad school were bifurcated. Many said that a strong liberal arts background would make for a well-rounded individual who then opts to enter the field of business—as part of a family business school, as a hired gun, or as an entrepreneur. Others felt that having a technical degree, in engineering or computer science for instance, would be of greater benefit in business school.

This has changed somewhat over more recent years for one compelling reason: The student of today has been told, and has recognized, that some of the best preparation for business school happens off campus, through multiple internships during their sophomore and junior summers. Successful internships in the business world now often lead directly to job offers and permanent employment. But there is also great value for students who take internships in the philanthropic space, or in other not-for-profit worlds, and gain experience that will be highly applicable to a business career. There is no question that an internship with a company usually is easier to gain for an undergraduate business student who speaks the language of business more easily than a liberal arts or engineering major. But as companies have sought to build more diverse, flexible, multitalented work forces, prime business internships are no longer the exclusive realm of business students.

A significant change over the years is that the top MBA programs now require three to five years of work experience prior to accepting students. The main reason for that is to enrich the classroom learning for all the students. The MBA classes tend not to follow the format of a "talking head" addressing students but rather embrace Socratic discussion among the professor and students. It is an iterative learning process, where experience comes into play for all.

As a graduate student myself I had NO significant work experience prior to joining my MBA classmates. Therefore, as we analyzed three cases a day, struggling to come to some kind of conclusion and to answer the question "What should the CEO do?"—I had great difficulty contributing to the analytical discussion. I look back and see that I was a "net taker" in those classes. I could only listen and learn. I was not a "giver," as were those classmates who had worked for Deloitte, Bain Consulting, McKinsey, Mattel, Alcoa, and even the United States military. They had much to contribute to the building of the whole solution, and I benefited from their experience. Today's top MBA programs want to encourage that kind of "giving" from their students.

The more that undergraduate programs can build experiential learning into their curricula, the better. This learning can come about in many forms. Among Marshall undergrads, we had students working with honeybee farmers in rural Panama, helping them in their daily work, but also teaching them fundamental accounting so they could achieve sustainability as well as profits. We had students consulting with Los Angeles small businesses in blighted areas, helping them build websites, or use marketing tools, or get loans to keep them afloat. And we had students working with faculty members on their research, learning how theories were then put into practice. All of these varied learning experiences ultimately led students to graduate school.

With 168 hours in a week, and only 16 of those hours being spent in the classroom, how students spend the other 152 hours truly determines their path to success. As much as we professors might want to think otherwise, we all teach pretty much the same thing in each subject or discipline. There are only so many ways you can explain debits/credits, net present value, or discounted cash flow. Beyond the classroom, however, the opportunities to learn are literally endless. Schools need to focus on this piece of learning for their students and differentiate themselves from other institutions where it is downplayed or not offered. And students need to take advantage of such offerings—the experiences outside the classroom greatly assist in learning, in giving, in resume building, and in preparation for the future.

There is a growing movement at schools to bring liberal arts graduates into MBA programs, and that makes great sense, as such grads round out their business classes. They help in the classroom discussions especially when the topic touches upon "soft" subjects, such as dealing with employees and other stakeholders, or public policy issues, or social justice situations. Conversely, those students who get an undergraduate degree in business need to have taken some liberal arts courses, so they can develop their personal view of the world. In pursuing wider studies, they may come to see corporate, geographic, or demographic needs and niches in the world that they can fill with a start-up of their own.

Engineering graduates, on the other hand, bring strong analytical skills to the MBA programs. They are quick to understand how to plot the spreadsheets, with all the variables, or to develop a better product. This is critical for the study groups to evolve, and their skills are highly desirable. A student with an undergraduate degree in business is well served to have taken computer sciences courses, such as code writing. They may never write any code in their lives but need to understand what goes into doing that. Getting much further into the engineering world is difficult for these students, but they need to know that the skills students bring from that world are totally necessary.

How valuable is an MBA and should I get one? In general, my answers have always been "Very" and "Yes." The MBA degree is a degree that no one can take away from you once you have it, and it is another credential in a world that values credentials. Many things learned during that course of study are applicable to such varied walks of life that even if the graduate ultimately decides not to pursue a career in business, what was learned during those years will prove invaluable.

As dean, I frequently counseled students who were concerned about the value of an MBA or whether they even needed it, to get into the early years of their careers and see what they thought about the degree at that point. I was fairly sure that they would see colleagues with an advanced degree moving up the organization faster, especially in the field of consulting or investment banking. If it became clear that their industry of choice valued the MBA, then it was a degree worth pursuing. But I also pointed out that an MBA may require some sacrifice and might even feel like a step backward. If a student has graduated and is finally living on their own and making a nice salary, they are going to feel—justifiably so—that they are already building a life and career. The thought of returning to being a poor and struggling student may not have much appeal.

Things have begun to change a bit, however, as many young people live with parents during the early years of their career to save money, and then perhaps find that their parents will be willing to help with tuition for an advanced degree, or maybe the money they saved by living at home will go toward that. If a student looks at grad school tuition as an expense and an investment, they might see the following, for example:

Suppose you are currently making \$75,000 a year. Tuition for an MBA might be \$120,000. So over two years, you are sacrificing \$150,000 in income and spending another \$120,000. Let's say your starting salary out of business school is \$120,000—is it really worth \$270,000 to move the income needle up \$45,000 annually? This is where long-term thinking needs to come into play. You will move further up from \$120K, much faster than from \$75K, over the long run and will most likely be sooner eligible to move into some lucrative positions. Yes, the advanced degree is expensive, but it has great value. Some students opt for going to school at night to get an MBA and that keeps their salaries intact. Some actually have the option of getting the degree online, and more and more schools are offering those degrees—with the same rigor and expected workload.

Finally, there are those students for whom an MBA is not just in the cards. Maybe they are in an industry that does not value the advanced degree. Maybe they just don't want to go back to school. Maybe they are farther down the road of life, having married and had children, or having bought a home with their partner. When those variables come into the picture, the question of value is not as important as the question of viable alternatives, which can be equally strong, depending on the individual. I believe that if you want to get an MBA, you have a couple of choices to make:

- Is the ranking of the school important?
- Will that particular school help me with career options after I finish?

The top schools are the top schools, and about that, there is no discussion. If you can get into Stanford, Chicago, Kellogg, Wharton, or Harvard, you run, don't walk. If you cannot, your best choice is to go to the one physically located as close to where you see yourself living and working, and then start to build your network immediately. Most schools have good alumni networks all over the world, and you can use them to your benefit to find a position, to change to another company, and to learn about the city where you work. Alums are good about helping more recent graduates get settled into their new lives. If you ultimately want to work in a particular geographic location, you might just as well be an alum of their most prestigious institution, i.e., University of Washington in Seattle, or University of Virginia/Duke/Vanderbilt for the South, or the University of Texas/SMU for Dallas, Houston, or Austin.

If it is a specific industry that you are focused on, you need to truly be specific as to what works. A desire to get into the entertainment industry might see you at UCLA, USC, or New York University. The oil industry might see you at Rice. Politics or public policy studies lend themselves to Georgetown. All business schools have traditionally offered a mix of practical skill sets and a more theoretical approach to the economics of business. It's important that a business school not be confused with a technical school—it is not simply about job training. There is always a balance between practical and theoretical applications.

Understand that you may be asked to move at some time in your career, perhaps to wherever corporate headquarters are. Therefore, studying in Texas because you want to live in Dallas may be good in the short run, but if you are working for Eli Lilly, you will most likely wind up in Indianapolis. That would mean another decision—to move or not to move—farther down the road. So, take the job that appeals to you the most, regardless of where in the world it is. If a job fits your desires and talents, it is probably the right one for you.

All good business schools need to recognize that they are equipping their students not just to excel in the classroom but to be prepared for the real-world strains and stresses of the business environment they will be stepping into. With the sudden impact of artificial intelligence into our world, business schools have moved fast to adapt their teachings and to utilize AI to the maximum. Those who do the best at this will definitely have a leg up on their competition. While workplace trends and the shifting needs of the business world may have an effect on business school curricula, sometimes the specific actions of prominent executives can have a more direct and wide-ranging influence.

As the first woman CEO of Deloitte, serving from 2003 to 2011, **Sharon Allen** was a true trailblazer. She worked at a firm that hired so many accountants each year and turned over a very similar number each year as they left and moved on in their careers, and she saw the fact that there were just not enough woman accountants. Deloitte and other comparable firms were just not as accommodating to women as they could have been. Sharon took this as a challenge and proceeded to establish Deloitte as the premier corporate organization in America for females. She made the workplace conductive for women to want to come and be a part of it; to have children and be able to be a mom and an employee. Sharon and her team explored many thoughts about flexible hours and time off—not just maternity leave but time to take care of the children when needed—all of which gave a female accountant a chance to be a much better worker in the firm.

As Sharon built the firm up and they hired more and more female accountants, the reputation spread and grew. Within the firm, there were many groups throughout the organization in which women could sit down and talk to one another about any issues they might still have balancing being a mom and a full-time worker, and then brainstorm on how to overcome them. Sharon was a true visionary from the standpoint of building organizations for the other 50 percent of society and was then able to hire the best of the best to be able to bring them into the firm. Over and over again it's been shown that Deloitte's workforce has been exceptional in so many respects due to the fact that women are very comfortable working there and know they can move up the ranks to become partners in the firm.

I have to give Sharon a lot of credit for the fact that women started looking at accounting as a career when they may not have thought that way prior to Sharon's coming to Deloitte. So, she truly changed the landscape in American business. We all worked harder at our schools so that we had parity—just as many women business students as male business students. Business administration became a discipline that many women began to see as a viable career path and therefore wanted to study in that discipline and excel in that discipline, and they have. From Sharon's top-down initiatives at her firm, it's worked out very well for all of us involved in business education. I was proud in 2018 when the USC Marshall School of Business was the first MBA program to achieve parity in gender between males and females in the incoming class.

I do not suggest that MBAs are a "must" for everyone. I know one young USC undergraduate, **Gary Chen**, whose father wanted him to be an accountant. Gary was all torn up because he did not want to be an accountant—he wanted to pursue an MBA and become an investment banker. He was excited about the prospect of developing skills that would help him navigate the risks of the investment world, while his father wanted him to take the reliable, steadier path of accountancy. The student wanted me to help make his case to the father, but this was one of the situations where I felt I did not want to cross the boundaries between an academic and family member.

Instead, I told the father that I felt his son would be a huge success, whatever he pursued. I understood that investment banking was what the son wanted to do, and I understood that the father wanted him to pursue the solid profession of an accountant, but I wanted the father to understand that I felt his son was going to be a success regardless of which path he followed. That being the case, it seemed to me that this was the moment for his son to decide a path for himself. The dad asked, "Are you sure? I'm so nervous about his future." I told him there would probably never be a time when he wouldn't be nervous about his son's future—that's just part of the "dad" job description—but I had confidence that Gary would succeed at what he put his mind to. The father got it.

Gary graduated over fifteen years ago, and we keep in touch regularly. He decided against pursuing an MBA but found his own path into investment banking and is a gigantic success.

Business education is much more practical than a typical academic education at the university level in that it includes not just classroom education but also experiential education. There's learning in other countries so that one may experience how other countries work, explore what the infrastructure looks like in another country, and discover how the customs and the mores of that society affect business. Simply put, the best way to learn how to deal with businesses in other countries is to do business in other countries. For example, in the experiences I had working in Japan, I found that before you really could do any serious business you needed to make sure that you'd built your relationship with your partner on the other side. The Japanese executives I dealt with wanted to spend a number of meals (i.e., lunches and dinners) with me just to get to know me before they wanted to talk business at all and before they wanted to negotiate about anything. Whereas in China, I have found that they are much more practical and quicker to make decisions and much more aligned to the American business culture and the way it works. They wanted to do business right away.

If you have the opportunity to step into a regular business office as an intern, it is important to observe and understand the culture there: Are the employees in cubicles? Are they in offices that have doors and/or windows? What is the environment like and how does it connect to the work being done? What's the culture like in terms of what time people come to work and what time people go home? Do they take lunch at their desk, or do they go out together for lunch? Do they have a cup of coffee together in the morning, or a drink together at night? What you try to understand there as an intern is the way the organization works, who's in charge, how do your work your way up in the organization, and what are some of the key performance indicators that are important to management, so that you know where you can excel and work your way up the ladder. A student intern really needs to evaluate all of that while they're on board as a part of the workplace.

As for the work actually being done, it is always hoped that the company is looking for an intern to do some significant work and not just making coffee and copies. The interns coming from today's universities are very bright, and if you give them a project they catch on very quickly and they'll work hard and make that project something of value. The more an owner or manager can give an intern to do, the better. Every CEO has on their desk a pile of papers of things they want to get done but never seem to get around to. How to evaluate competition. Where would a new product fit? What new products might a firm want to look at, and what new markets might they want to look at? Those kinds of projects are very easy to turn over to an intern.

When I think of experiential learning, one particular classroom moment comes to mind. One of the most astute businessmen I know is **Tom Barrack**, the founder of Colony Capital, a major real estate firm in Southern California. Tom came from a Lebanese grocery family where he lived over the grocery store and he worked in the store, so he learned the value of hard work, discipline, and work ethic. Those values were deeply instilled within him as he developed his own career.

Tom—a USC grad—was honored by the university's Entrepreneurship program and had the opportunity to spend some time with students before he accepted the award. He was so direct and straightforward with them. One student asked, "If you were me, what would you be doing right now preparing yourself for your career?" Tom's answer was quick and succinct. He didn't suggest a particular class, or a particular major, or a particular job-hunting strategy. He suggested getting some world experience. What he said specifically was, "If I were you, I'd be in China right now." And today, he might answer that question differently, reflecting the flexibility of a strong business mind.

Tom's understanding of global business is virtually unparalleled. He understands how the Middle East works—so well that he was asked to be the US ambassador to Turkey—as well as how Asia works, how Europe works; and his suggestion to that student was right on the money. At the time, China was opening up markets and was a place where someone needed to be in order to understand exactly what they were doing. So, business education is way more than formal education.

Some of the finest business teachers are not necessarily business school professors. If one considers that perhaps the most crucial lessons a young entrepreneur can learn are centered on the art of leadership, then it follows that those lessons may come from anyone who has experience as a leader. **General David Petraeus** does not hold an MBA (though he does have a PhD in international relations from Princeton's Woodrow Wilson School), and he is known for a stellar military career rather than any business experience. Nevertheless, it would be hard to find someone with greater insight into the responsibilities and rewards for strong leadership.

My first meeting with the general came as we walked from my office to a classroom where he would address a room full of students working to achieve a Master's in Business for Veterans—all students being either military veterans or those currently serving—the first for business schools to offer. As we walked, I asked him if we could take a slight detour for him to talk to our Marshall School Board of Leaders. For fifteen minutes, without notes, he took all of us on a tour of the world's hot spots, in a very detailed, unflinching description of the stakes at hand in each conflict zone, leaving us stunned and speechless.

We then walked to the veterans' classroom, and at the door, he asked me, "Where do you think you are going?" Taken by surprise, I responded that I was going in to listen to him. He said that there was absolutely no way I could do that—this was a talk between the students and him. Needless to say, when a five-star general tells you that there's something you cannot do, you don't do it!

From what I heard through students later, they were deeply impressed with the general's presentation. For almost three hours, he talked with students about his career. He admitted to and took full responsibility for his mistakes throughout his career—the sign of a leader who has been called one of the best military battle captains in our country's history.

**Questions About Your Own Education:**

- As you finish school and move into the real world, what continuing education topics would you like to pursue?
- What knowledge would help you directly in pursuing your career?
- What would help in your personal development?
- What would simply be a pleasure for you to learn about?
- Do you understand the business side of your current career, or do you need more education in this regard?
- What have you done to continue lifelong learning, such as a graduate degree, classes at a local institution of higher learning, or even just in-depth reading about topics?
- If you could design your own MBA program, mixing practical, theoretical, and experiential learning, what would it look like?

# Chapter 4

# Relationships and Mentors

## *The Power of Connection*

When very successful people are asked how they were able to attain such lofty perches in their lives and careers, many will strike a note of humility and answer that their achievements were made possible by standing on the shoulders of the giants that went before them. Those achievements were also greatly facilitated by the family members, friends, and close acquaintances who walked side by side with them along the way. And many of these close acquaintances come about through the networking that we do during the course of our lives.

Truly the finest networker I've met is a gentleman named **Steve Silk**. Steve is one of the most likable guys I have ever known, and he endears himself to everyone. As a principal of Eastdil Secured, a significantly sized real estate firm, he is always working to see if there is a deal to be had somewhere in the room. One of Steve's greatest networking talents is that he operates by the Socratic method rather than the hard sell—that is, rather than pitching himself, he knows how to ask the right questions to get you talking. In a setting where there may be potential business connections, Steve will ask lots of questions about the industry somebody represents, questions about a company's position within that industry, and specific questions about projects that the company may have. It is Steve's superpower that people don't feel "interrogated" by him—they are flattered that he's so interested in what they do.

Ultimately, Steve is the kind of connection-savvy power broker who will put a buyer and seller together and voila!—a deal is struck, Eastdil making the commission on it. More often than not, though, Steve might suggest that "Party A" should call "Party B" and talk about something that "Party A" is working on and needs help with. He is not just looking to get a deal done—he's mostly driven by the urge to bring people together in a way that will be mutually beneficial to both parties.

Steve is constantly on the move but seems to be a ubiquitous presence to those who know him. He shows up at events to listen to speakers and to learn, but he will work the crowd himself if the opportunity presents itself. He has a wonderful memory for names and situations, which means that the second time you meet him, you feel he has already developed a personal connection with you.

I felt connected enough to Steve to invite him to become an adjunct professor for real estate at USC. Steve worked with the top students who wanted to go into the field of real estate, and his gift for communication had a brand-new showcase. He was in a situation where there was no actual "deal" to be made beyond his sharing expertise and experience with hungry young minds. Steve has excelled at this and become a mentoring figure to many of his students.

I've already indicated that I was in the unique position of having two family members—father and father-in-law—as mentors, but in the position of dean I was able to observe these kinds of relationships develop between faculty and students.

My definition of a good mentor is someone who has been where you might like to go, and who is serving in that mentorship capacity in such a manner that you are their only agenda. They don't stand to benefit from the relationship other than to see you become a success. They are objective, thoughtful, and caring in their approach to you and your questions. They are generous with their time.

I often encouraged students and recent graduates to seek out these relationships, but I frequently found that I would have to explain how a mentorship happens. Students, as smart as they were, sometimes seemed to think that they could just walk into a professor's office and ask the professor straight out to be their mentor! Doesn't quite work that way. It is very much an evolutionary process. It takes time for two people to come to know one another's strengths, weaknesses, foibles, idiosyncrasies, visions, and goals. It takes time for a student to recognize how much they may be able to learn from someone wiser—so much more than what is presented in a classroom or at a job orientation. And it takes time for a potential mentor to recognize the potential for growth in a student or young employee.

Once the mentor and student recognize the potential in each other, it becomes a very active relationship. What a mentor offers a student can shift as the student grows. In my case, my father gave me a basic understanding of business and customer service when I was quite young. As I went into business for myself, he was able to mentor me in the finer points of customer service and time management—I didn't outgrow his expertise.

That can happen, though, so it is important to remember that the mentor relationship isn't necessarily an exclusive one. Your mentors can change as you move through your career and turn to different figures for guidance and instruction. Just keep in mind that if you get to the point where you think you know everything—you probably haven't thought about it hard enough.

Throughout my business/academic career, nothing has been more satisfying than talking with young people and guiding them through decisions relative to their careers and their personal lives. I have always tried to avoid ever saying "You should . . . ," instead asking them questions like "Have you considered . . ." or "Would something like _____ be of interest?" Asking probing questions rather than making bold statements that reflect my own prejudices seemed to work much better, as the young people ultimately have to live with their decisions—I don't.

There is never one right answer to the questions that they have when we meet, but rather some answers that are better than others.

**Amanda Levine** was a brilliant freshman when we first met. She was ambitious, and in introducing herself to her classmates that first day of class, she stated emphatically that she was going to graduate from Harvard Business School and be an investment banker—a statement she never wavered from.

She interned with Goldman Sachs between her junior and senior years and was offered a full-time position in their Los Angeles office. A couple of years after she had graduated, she called me, wanting to talk. The long, arduous hours were taking their toll on her and giving her no social life whatsoever. She asked what she should do. When I asked her what her successful businessman father said, she answered: "Do what Professor Ellis says to do."

I could tell in that phone call that she was nearing the breaking point, saying that it seemed she should resign immediately or risk a nervous breakdown. Her retort was that if she did, she would never get to Harvard. I thought otherwise and told her that there were many avenues that led to Cambridge.

She did leave the firm, and in fact the whole industry, and took a position within the entertainment business. A couple of years later, she called with another dilemma: "I have been accepted at Harvard Business School and the Anderson School at UCLA for my graduate studies in business, and don't know what to do." My flip answer, "What's his name?," brought dead silence on the other end. I had to explain that the decision to attend her long-time dream school should be quite easy unless a young man she was involved with did not want her to go back East. I think she was shocked that I could come to the conclusion so quickly that the decision had to do with more than just a choice of school.

I asked if she had been to Cambridge. She had not but was scheduled to go for a visit soon. I asked her to call me when she returned from that trip. She did, admitting, "OK, I get it now—it would be completely wrong to turn down an HBS offer to then stay in Los Angeles." I agreed, making the bold statement that the fellow in question might be gone by November anyway!

Her Harvard experience was terrific, and she made the most of her two years there. The romance that had seemed to be such a big factor did indeed fade away. She returned to Southern California to a job in the consumer goods business, happy and pleased with her decisions—all of which she had made on her own. I had only been there to listen and to question. She made all the decisions.

Another opportunity for mentorship arose when I met a high school senior from New York City, **Sophia Doyle**, who visited our campus with her mother and came in to see me. She was ready to go to Georgetown—it was on the East Coast where she grew up and was comfortable—unless she was admitted to a special USC program where she could study abroad for her sophomore and junior years, receiving three college degrees from three universities and on three continents—our very successful World Bachelor in Business.

I did not think she would be admitted to that program but saw great promise in this young student and worked hard to talk her into giving a regular USC business degree serious consideration. She left my office telling her mom that she wanted to matriculate at USC, at the same time that my assistant said to me, "That young lady would be a perfect USC student!" That is exactly what she turned out to be.

Time and again, I would look up from my desk to see her standing outside my office window with five fingers in the air—"Can I have five minutes of your time?" She had figured out how to work around the gatekeepers in my office to get directly to me!! We talked about many career opportunities for her, analyzing the interviews she had and was going to have, and after a very successful four years, she took a position in San Francisco with an investment firm, where she did very well. That, however, is not the end of the story.

She married a longtime boyfriend of Austrian descent—Gail and I attended their wedding in Vienna—and the two of them had to resist his family's wanting him to return to Austria to work in the family business. They came back to the Bay Area, where he continued his consulting career, and she decided to start a business teaching financial literacy to girls.

Did my many happy hours of mentoring lead her to this start-up idea? No, but it gave her a chance to talk through whatever was on her mind and to be creative in her thoughts. THAT is what led to her starting the company. Today she has started something else: a family! And as of this writing, they live in Milan, Italy, and are doing great!!

A mentoring opportunity that I did not want nor even expect came my way one Monday morning when I was quietly sitting at my office desk at the school. I looked up, and one of my students was sitting right there in front of me—I had not even heard her come in. She just said, "Hi," and I asked her what she was doing there. Students NEVER show up in a professor's office at 9 a.m. on a Monday!

Melanie (not her real name) was an unusual student—she had come in many times to talk about her future, always with questions and creative thoughts. She was a bundle of energy in these conversations, and I enjoyed the banter that took place as we strategized her future. She had had a difficult childhood but was exceptionally bright and was able to make good decisions.

This particular morning, though, she was somber and introspective and proceeded to tell me that she had been date-raped over the weekend at a party. I asked if she knew the boy, and she did. After she had given me all the details, and even some I didn't need to know, I asked her a couple of key questions:

"What did the police say when you reported it?" A blank stare returned.

"What did your parents say when you told them?" Again . . . blank.

"Who have you told?"

"YOU."

Uh-oh, I was worried this was going to be a problem. I was trained in business, not psychology, and certainly not in this arena. It was pretty obvious that I was going to be over my head if I tried to do anything other than get her to the right people, which is what I did.

I walked her to the Health Services clinic, where the doctor came out to get her. She insisted that I go into his office with her, but I had to draw the line and tell her I would wait outside, but that I would be there when she came out. The doctor verified that she had indeed been raped and the incident was reported properly.

Melanie and I did not talk the remainder of the semester, her final one as a student. The next time I saw her was in Seattle, as I was about to give my first talk to alumni in the area. She walked right up in front of me and, again, just said, "Hi." I asked her what she was doing there, and she responded that she had come to see me. She wanted me to meet her fiancé and she introduced him to me. The three of us chatted for a while before I had to begin my talk, and I got the impression that she had found a soulmate who understood what she had been through and felt as least as protective of her as I did.

The next communication I received from them was a year and half later—a birth announcement of their first child. She had moved on, successfully, and now was responsible for the life of a little person. I could not have been prouder of that, given all we had talked about and all she had shared with me. Faced with a terrible circumstance, she had gone on to find strength, success, and love.

**Mentoring takes all forms—be prepared.**

**Questions About Your Relationships:**

- Do you feel you have a strong network of friends who understand you and support you?
- How would you describe the different feelings you have for people you are close to in different settings: family, friendships, school, work?
- Is it easy for you to connect with people who interest you?
- What could you do to develop this skill?
- Not counting parents, have you had a mentor?
- What could you do to develop this skill?
- Why might you need a mentor at your stage of life?
- Where could that mentor help you?

# Chapter 5

# Plotting Your Own Map

## *Know Thyself*

Mentors can help you make good decisions for yourself. But creating a road map for your career depends on the Delphic maxim "Know thyself." First, you must know your limits—no matter how convinced you are that you can achieve anything. Second, in a world filled with distracting temptations and glitter, you must hold on to yourself above all else. Only by knowing your own character can you try and improve the way you make right and ethical decisions.

The world of politics may not jump to mind when one thinks of ethics or bridled ambition, but I had the occasion to meet two of our country's great political leaders, each of whom exhibited principles of restraint and acute self-awareness. As the political field began to take shape for the presidential election of 1988, **Senator Sam Nunn** of Georgia was being wooed by my father-in-law to run for president, with the promise that he, Bob Galvin, would bring a large number of Republican CEOs to support this Democratic candidate.

Bob asked Gail and me to join him for lunch with the senator, which we happily did. As he talked with Sam about a potential campaign, it was quite obvious that the senator was reluctant. Finally, Sam said to Bob something I will never forget: "I just don't want to put my family through what it takes to run for the top office in the land." Here was a man turning down the opportunity to be supported in a candidacy for president based on his love of family and his hesitancy toward making their lives miserable during the process.

The senator was honest, calm, and strong in his decision not to run for that reason. He acknowledged that he could do the job, and there was no reason to doubt that, but he did not want it. We all had to respect that decision completely.

On the same day that we had had lunch with Senator Nunn, we had evening cocktails with Texas Senator **Lloyd Bentsen** and his wife at the Galvin home. Bob told Lloyd what he had asked Senator Nunn and then asked Senator Bentsen the same thing: Would he consider running for the presidency if he knew he had upwards of fifty CEOs behind him?

Senator Bentsen replied in an equally thoughtful manner: "Bob, I just don't think I have the charisma to be the president. It requires a good deal of personality and someone who is of an extroverted nature, and that is just not me." Now there was a man who knew his strengths and weaknesses and was not afraid to talk about them. He was honest and forthright with his assessment and—speaking of questions of charisma—sometime later Bentsen would be the one to say to Dan Quayle during a vice president debate, "Senator, I knew Jack Kennedy. You're no Jack Kennedy." A wonderful man with a great wit.

When working for a university as the dean of admissions, one walks a fine line between academic standards and the harsh reality that a college is a business endeavor with limited resources. Do you admit students based solely on grade point average and test scores? Do you let recommendations sway your thinking? How much do outside activities come into play during the decision-making process? Do you let someone in just because they are a member of a family with a dozen supportive alums from your university? Do you admit the child of a large donor based on how much money the parent contributed to the school over the years?

**Katharine Harrington** often had to handle those questions at USC. As dean of admissions at a private university, she had more latitude in her decisions, but she still had to strike a balance between the academic excellence of the institution and the financial health of the institution. She had been a professor in the Marshall School of Business prior to moving to university admissions, so she knew how to reach a good outcome. She also had her PhD in ethics, so she was well suited for the post.

During the time we worked together, I never saw her make a misstep in this perilous territory. Decisions were ethical and honest. If she felt a student did not belong in the incoming freshman class, she told them so, and if they really wanted to come to USC, she helped them with a possible alternate path. As we discussed many times, "No one has ever asked you where you started college, but rather where you finished." Transferring from a junior college or another four-year university still allowed the student to graduate from USC, and Katharine would explain those options in such a manner that the student knew admission still was not guaranteed—but a possibility. Katharine wanted to see that they could perform at a college level. If they could and did well at it, their options opened up.

The college admissions process has come under great scrutiny in these last few years and rightfully so. There is so much pressure on high school students to perform so they can get into an elite American university, and this goes for international students as well. Parents have tried everything they can to get their kids into what they think is the right school to the point that some are willing to cut corners to make it happen. Ethical dilemmas exist everywhere.

While the process of admitting students is certainly more of an art than a science, Katharine was able to keep it as much a science as possible. She knew the data points that could come close to predicting success at the college level, and she knew where she had some subjectivity in making the decision. She did keep the firewall up between admissions and fundraising.

Having parameters to work under—guidelines if you will—helped her a great deal in doing her work. Beyond the available data points, she was very aware that some students will bloom later in life, or later in their college careers, and some students may have winning traits that may not be immediately obvious on their application. Katharine developed a great sense for who would succeed, and she could make the decisions to admit or not, and sleep with those decisions, knowing she had made the best ones she could under the circumstances.

"Get it in writing" is probably never bad advice in the business world, but I've been surprised (and impressed, really) to see how often in business a level of personal trust is just as important as signed contracts. One of the greatest examples I can recall of someone whose trustworthiness was key to their business dealings is **Martha Marcon**, who began her career as an accountant with KPMG.

In 1961 George Joseph founded Mercury General Insurance and built it into a relatively significant low-cost provider of automobile insurance, beginning in the California market and later branching out into many other states around the country. Mr. Joseph set up a board when his company went public, and a number of years later in 2016, he brought Martha onto the board. Martha was elevated to the position of independent lead director of the board, chiefly because she had achieved a great level of trust between her, Mr. Joseph, and the CEO of the company.

It's all about trust. No matter how big the company, executives and board members have to feel that decisions are being made ethically, honestly, and transparently. If they don't all trust that company's decision-making process, the process crumbles. Martha is thoughtful and understands the workings of the insurance industry and the workings of Mercury, and she makes decisions based on what is best for the company. As a leader, she had been very creative, but the critical bond of trust between the board and the company was never sacrificed.

Any board has to understand how their company makes its decisions, and why the company is making those decisions. Martha, with her background in general accounting procedures, understands the financials of the insurance industry and she relies on her expertise to engender trust from all parties, be it her fellow directors or the VPs of the company. She has worked hard on emphasizing the trust factor and has earned the trust of everyone who collaborates with her.

Martha developed the trust of Mr. Joseph through continuity of involvement. She had been involved with Mercury General since 1984, either as an auditor or director, and he was able to see how she thought about the issues of the company. In either role, her recommendations were just that—recommendations—and not decisions that had to be made. That was for the company officers. She just kept the company first in her thought process and built recommendations around that.

Time is not the only way to build trust, but it helps. In taking over as the leader of Motorola from his father who founded the business, Bob Galvin always said that the most difficult thing he had to do on the job was to know that his father trusted him. He was given the "keys to the kingdom" on the basis of trust and had to perform to that level.

Trust became so important in the Galvin family that my wife designed a medallion with a *T* for trust in the center of it. The four hands represent her and her siblings, and the oak leaves around the edge are for Rolling Oaks Farm, where they were raised. Everything centered on trust.

Our kids, Bob's grandchildren, when they turned twenty-one were allowed to use the medallion in any way they wished. Some made theirs to be worn around the neck, some made them as watch faces, some as rings. As parents, we were given the medallion when our last child turned twenty-one, and I had mine made into cuff links. Reminders of the importance of trust.

Shareholders buy stock in companies because they trust the management and leadership of the business to do things the right way. Customers buy products because they trust the company that manufactured the product to make it with quality. FedEx used to advertise that they would have the package to us "absolutely, positively overnight, by 10:30 the next morning" to build our trust in them—and when they could not make that happen EVERY time, they stopped saying it.

Parents send their children to a particular school because they trust that the school will take care of them. In my role as dean, I know that we were being entrusted with the greatest asset of a family—their children—to educate them in the best way we knew how and to keep them out of harm's way.

If you cannot trust your boss, and many of us cannot, I would say that is not a place where you should work. At some time, they will throw you under the bus to advance their own agenda—I have seen this happen time and again. Or, you may say something to a coworker in confidence and they violate that trust to gain goodwill for themselves in a situation—not good to either share your thoughts or even work in that environment.

Sometimes personal success will put you in a position where others feel tempted to judge you, assuming that you must have done something unethical to achieve your success. Perhaps you'll know you've done nothing wrong, but sometimes even the whisper of unethical behavior is enough to bring on consequences as if it really had happened. It is very perplexing and tormenting to be suspected of unethical actions you did not take, and extremely difficult to defend your hard-earned reputation in such a circumstance.

I first came to know **Tim Sloan** well when our sons played on the same Little League team at the age of about eleven. We volunteered to be the two coaches of the team.

Living in the same town, we saw each other at social events and stayed connected with each other's career. Tim worked for Wells Fargo Bank, bringing a strong work ethic to the job and helping to build the bank into a great West Coast institution. I always had the impression that he was one of those people who worked hard, stayed out of the limelight, and gave credit for success to others. And I knew from our days on the baseball diamond that he was as honest as the day is long.

Tim worked hard, built a great corporate team, developed great leadership skills, and ultimately came to head a division of the company that was very successful. Unfortunately, another division of the bank endured some very painful and unethical decision-making by its leadership. It came to the attention of the regulators of the banking industry, the investment community, and then the Congress of the United States. The CEO of the bank was called into a Senate committee hearing, where he was reprimanded harshly for the actions of the bank, and he was asked by his board of directors to resign.

Tim Sloan was named the CEO of the bank. Very quickly he was summoned to the same Senate committee, where he too was chastised publicly—this time by Senator Elizabeth Warren of Massachusetts. She told him in no uncertain terms that he should be fired. While this played out in the media, those of us who knew Tim knew that he did not deserve this. He had to take the beating for errors made by people who had not even reported to him.

His subsequent stepping away from the post and retiring from the bank was the ultimate act of taking one for the team. He had not done anything in his career that would have smacked of unethical behavior, and yet he was being punished for such behavior by others. Never have I respected someone more for the manner in which he handled himself as he went out the door—head held high, for he knew he had personally done nothing wrong. He had always been true to his values right to the end.

If you have a job you love doing, it doesn't really feel like work. But how do you get that job?

I like to say you "create" the path of your own career rather than "follow" one because, frankly, that path doesn't exist until you start moving out in the real world and plotting your own course. You can know where you want to go careerwise and know where you're headed at any particular moment, but I counseled graduating Marshall students again and again to leave room for exploration and surprise in their careers—which in turn means leaving some room for failure and happenstance. Especially these days, the idea that someone entering the business world will find the right job at the right company and keep at it for thirty or forty years before retiring is no longer reality based. The job market and business climate are more dynamic than ever, so let your career path adapt to what's out there and to what is most likely to be satisfying work for you.

When I first graduated from business school, I had already given up my dream of being a professional golfer. But golf still managed to impact my career. I first came to Southern California not because I had a hot job prospect but because I knew the better weather would allow me more time on the greens than I would get in the Boston area. After some rounds of interviews, I got a job with The Broadway department stores. I was recruited and hired by a true gentleman named **Phil Hawley** who at that point was president of The Broadway, and who still ranks as one of the people I most respect out of all the people I have come across in my career.

I wasn't hired with much of a specific portfolio to attend to, because it had been some years since a Harvard MBA had joined the firm. I remember Phil saying, "I don't know what to do with you, but you'll figure it out." He wanted me to understand the workings of the entire company, so he put me with our vice president of operations, who started me in the warehouse unloading boxcars and sorting through piles of merchandise! I worked through the receiving and distribution areas and then headed out to store operations. Two years of this seemed to round me out as a trainee, and I was then deemed ready for merchandising. As Phil said, "It is good to start at the beginning and understand how an organization and its people work."

So, I got a sense of how the company worked and where I could fit in, and then was named a buyer in the merchandising department. After ten years, when I began to feel I had learned all I could from The Broadway and began to look around for my next opportunity, I encountered some important lessons about career development.

I left The Broadway in 1979 to go work for Miller's Outpost—a very fast-growing chain of young men's and women's jeans and casual apparel stores. I was in charge of the entire men's area of the store, and I had a boss who as it turned out was not a particularly great communicator in terms of his own philosophy and strategy. That said, we were quite successful mainly because the chain was on a great growth track and things were going very well. As we said many times, "Sales volume cures all ills!"

However, at one point I sat down with him and came to find out that he didn't agree with my merchandising strategy. I was trying to sell more higher-priced items than he wanted to do. He wanted to specialize in lower-priced items that we could put on sale for even lower prices and was primarily interested in moving lots of volume rather than building a reputation for quality. We went back and forth for a while, but the end result was that he asked me to leave the company. There was no acrimony—we just had a difference in philosophy that couldn't be reconciled. He said, "You can stay as long as you want until you find a new job."

As I left Miller's that day, I got in my car and started crying—I really was panicked. Here I was, thirty-two years old, a Harvard MBA, and soon to be unemployed. I didn't know which way to turn. I decided to call my old boss at The Broadway, who had told me that I would come to him one day because he didn't think I would enjoy a specialty store business like Miller's Outpost. I hadn't understood that at the time—I'd been flattered to be hired away by another company. But now as I was driving home, I sort of figured out that he had been right.

I called him when I got home and I said, "I am out of a job, and I would really like to know if there's something I can do to come back to The Broadway." At that point he couldn't resist saying something along the lines of "I told you so." Then he said he would think things over and get back to me. He gave me a call a couple of days later on a Friday afternoon at five fifteen and said, "I have an opportunity. I've got a division I'd really like you to lead for us and take it and run with as you see fit. I can pay you a hundred thousand dollars a year."

At the time I was making $150,000 a year, but I had just been fired from that job so therefore I was currently making zero—and a $100,000 job at a company I knew very well sounded pretty good. So, I said OK.

Before he got back to me, though, I'd been making some calls trying to set up some interviews—because I was panicking. I really didn't have much of a cushion of finances to fall back on. I was a young, single guy with a house and a mortgage, and I was pretty nervous that my severance from Miller's Outpost would run out quickly. Then I would be with no income.

I made a number of calls and set up some interviews—just in case The Broadway didn't want me back. I'd set up an interview for Monday morning at eight o'clock with Mervyn's stores in

Northern California and when I got The Broadway's job offer late Friday afternoon, I immediately tried to call Mervyn's to cancel my appointment, but they were already gone for the day. This was before there were cell phones and email, so I had no means by which to contact the man I was going to be interviewing with. I made the decision that I would make the trip up north and go ahead with the interview, and at some point, I would tell them I already had a job offer back home. Sunday night, I flew up to Hayward, California, on the east side of San Francisco Bay and met with the Mervyn's people at eight o'clock Monday morning. They had a whirlwind day planned for me that ended at about four o'clock. During the entire time, the moment never felt right to say a word about the fact that I had another job offer.

I got on the airplane to head back south and thought, "OK, that was a nice day but it's not going to culminate in any kind of offer, and I'll be fine." That night at about eight o'clock the senior vice president of human relations at Mervyn's called me and said, "Jim, we were interviewing you for a divisional merchandise manager's job, but we've decided you're overqualified for that job and we've decided to make a few moves and offer you a vice president's job. The salary that we're offering you is four hundred thousand dollars a year." I gulped and thought to myself, "Uh-oh," and said, "Thank you—let me get back to you tomorrow."

Now what's the first thing that a thirty-two-year-old single man would do when confronted with such a dilemma? Call Dad.

I called my father and explained the two offers and the two different opportunities, and he asked, "So the one offered you a hundred thousand and the other offered you four hundred thousand dollars?" I said, "Yes."

And he asked, "What did you tell the first company?" I said that I had told them I'd take the job.

"Then why are you calling me?" Dad asked.

"Well, Dad, four hundred minus one hundred is three hundred. That's a big difference."

"Why did you call me again? What did you tell the first company?"

"Dad—I told them I'd take the job."

"Then I don't understand the call. The only thing you have in your life is your reputation and your word. If you go back on your word it will catch up with you."

I said, "You are really not being a good help to me at all, Dad—thank you very much. Goodbye."

I hung up—and I knew he was right. I had made the decision too quickly and accepted the $100,000 job, and all of a sudden something that was far more lucrative had come along. I really had put myself in a bind. I had to realize and acknowledge that I had already accepted the first job. I needed to honor my word.

Early on, every decision made in regard to your career is a building block, and those blocks are set one on top of another to become the foundation that allows you to construct whatever kind of career you want. I surely would have enjoyed the extra $300,000 a year back then, but I am glad that at a crucial crossroads—with a nudge from my father—I made the integrity of my word a foundational building block of my career. Reputation, and protecting it, would truly come into play in my life many years later.

Early in my career at The Broadway—as part of my all-around training—I was told to report to **Joe Lopez** on the receiving dock for two weeks of experience there. When I met Joe, I encountered a hugely imposing figure. Literally. Joe was probably six foot six and 275 pounds, with bushy hair and a beard, and he took great pride in the fact that he drove the biggest motorcycle in the parking lot. I'd been intimidated by some of my Harvard professors, but Joe was in a whole different category of scary.

Joe asked me if I knew how to drive a forklift truck, to which I responded, "No, sir. Not at all." He had one of the warehouse workers teach me the basics of the lift in a few short minutes and then sent me out to unload the pallets coming in on a railroad car outside. It had been one hundred degrees inside that car, and my forklift was certainly not air conditioned! I unloaded boxcars for five days straight, wearing a tie (which Joe would not permit me to take off—"You are a trainee, so deal with it") in one-hundred-plus-degree heat and developed a lasting appreciation for the work of the receiving dock crew.

In my second week on the dock, Joe gave me a new assignment, this time—mercifully—indoors. I was to help a woman named Maria in the task of sorting patent leather handbags by color. The vendor had shipped them to us in bulk, and we needed to separate and organize them so they could be easily stocked in the stores. Maria had me sit down on the floor next to her, surrounded by a mountain of handbags and a bunch of empty boxes. We were to throw the bags into the boxes by color—there were about eight different shades.

After about an hour of this tedious work, I casually said to Maria, as any good Harvard MBA grad might, "There must be an easier way to do this." She responded sharply, "I have been doing this for ten years, and there is not. So shut up and keep sorting." Ouch—she certainly put me in my place. I spent the next hour sorting and racking my brain for what the better system might be, and she was right—there wasn't a better way, except for maybe having someone else do it.

As I worked my way through The Broadway's training program, I was tasked with moving merchandise through our service center and out to our forty-plus stores. That's when I encountered **Adele Soffa**, a women's wear buyer. It seemed to me that Mrs. Soffa's department was not as thorough and quick in processing paperwork as other departments. So, taking the initiative, one day I walked into her office and confronted her assistants with the fact that I needed the appropriate paperwork to move some goods to the trucks immediately. She heard me giving the assistants a hard time and yelled out from her inner office: "Who the hell is out there? Get in here."

I had heard she was tough but did not know how tough until I took the brunt of her yelling. I would not back down, though, and told her that she and her team were wrong in this situation—I needed to get those dresses out of the building to make room for incoming shipments. She stopped yelling long enough to query, "Who are you, and where did you come from?" When I calmly answered her, she settled down and we began to talk. It became obvious to her that even though I was a trainee, I had a job to do and was just trying to do it well. And I think she also recognized that I was not just trying to be annoying to her and that I cared about doing a good job for the company as much as she did.

Shortly after the first meeting, Adele invited me to lunch with one of her largest suppliers just so I could see how the fast-moving women's wear world worked. It was fascinating listening to her in action, as she asked him question after question about the business trends around the country, what was next, and what was or wasn't working in the stores. She was gaining knowledge that would help her with ordering merchandise in the next months and what pitfalls she should avoid. She also negotiated some terms—price/discounts/ship dates/colors—in a firm and very positive manner.

As we drove home from lunch, we reviewed what had transpired. She talked about what she had wanted to accomplish in that meeting and where she had succeeded in getting what she wanted and what she left on the table. I had learned in business school that negotiating is about many topics, not just price, and that you should leave your most important issue until later in the conversation, when you see where the supplier's weaknesses are. I don't know where or whether Adele had studied, but she was a master tactician.

Over the next years, Adele included me in many meetings, often letting me ask questions and always encouraging me to listen carefully to what was said around a negotiating table. After every one of those meetings, we did a debrief on what had happened and what was achieved. She became a terrific mentor in teaching me the ways of getting what you needed in the business to become a success.

**Matthew Guglielmo** had been a furniture buyer with a Philadelphia department chain before venturing west to move up The Broadway's corporate ladder. He had a great eye for detail in sofas, chairs, tables, and lamps that gave him a keen edge over his competitors. And when he became a supervisor of a group of Broadway buyers, that eye for detail served him well in his training of them. That's where I came into the picture. Matt was essentially my boss's boss, so while I did not have direct contact with him on a daily basis, I had enough to learn a lot from him. I will never forget receiving a memo from Matt, telling us that we needed to be sure to include our telephone extension in all our communications with others to make it easier for them to communicate back to us. No detail was too small to not be attended to and shame on you if you did not pay attention to it.

Matt taught me how to prepare for negotiations by knowing what I wanted and knowing when to ask for all of it. His philosophy was that you may not get everything you want, but if you don't ask for all of it, you surely won't get it. Set your objectives for your meetings with vendors, just as Adele Soffa had suggested, and make sure that you include anything and everything that would benefit you and your goals.

Matt and I worked together for a number of years, and I was always learning from him. Though he was higher up the ladder than I was, he had a great habit of asking me questions to see where I stood on a variety of issues confronting our business, and he was always interested in hearing how I planned to move the business forward. The fact that he took my ideas and opinions seriously really had an effect on me and stretched me in many ways, such that I was able to succeed beyond where I might have thought possible.

Learning from the ground up is invaluable when you are beginning a career, as it gives you great respect for those who do the jobs that make a business run, and for those whose work supports your own work. I can't help but think that was a part of what my father wanted to convey to me when he'd take me to his bank on Saturday and let me pick a spot to sit at—teller's station, loan officer's desk, VP's office. The idea was that a bank or any business succeeds on the strength of a variety of workers doing a variety of jobs and the better understanding you have of that, the better the odds for your own success.

**Put yourself in the shoes (or purses or forklifts) of those who work around you.**

An earlier boss of mine was a New York rug merchant named **Fred Kramer**. He was a very serious guy who had a wonderfully dry sense of humor. I learned the best of the retail business from

Fred in the years I worked for him, with many of the concepts spilling over into my academic years as well.

Fred taught me that you ALWAYS need to keep some "dry powder"—some funds in reserve to use during difficult times to either bail yourself out or take advantage of opportunities that invariably exist during those times. With that in mind, I set up reserve accounts where I stashed money on a regular basis, so I could participate in advantageous purchases when they came up. And while I know Fred's advice was primarily meant for my role as a merchandise buyer, the concept of setting aside some reserve "dry powder" is applicable to anything in life.

Fred also kept me on my toes when it came to my numbers—the profit and loss statement of my individual department. After we worked together, I made sure during every phase of my career that I had a strong working knowledge of the financial situation. Success does not come from guessing, but from knowing where you stand at all times.

Finally, Fred taught me how to be creative as a merchant. He wanted me not just to buy what was offered by the market but also embellish it a bit, so our customer was given that much more for the price. The importance of creativity in any business situation was formed during this experience and has never been forgotten.

On the other side of the buying-selling relationship, one of the greatest salespeople to come across my path was **Jim Flood**, an inventor of the graphite golf shaft and the Basakwerd putter, of which we sold thousands in a short time. Jim could sell anything to anyone.

He once told me that he would list the positives and the negatives of a product/service on the page and then tear up that half of the page with negative aspects. Only focus on the positive, he told me, and don't drive yourself crazy with what could happen.

Stories about Jim's sales abilities were rampant and extended beyond the workplace. There was one about the time he forgot to pay the electric bill at home. When his wife came home that night, he was on the porch waiting for her and quickly suggested that they go to the movies. She insisted on getting a wrap and went inside to a dark house. Coming out, she asked why they were going to the movies when they had no electricity and needed to deal with that problem. His answer: "We will go out and when we return, it will be time for bed when we need dark. We will wake up tomorrow and the sun will light the house." There were no negative thoughts there.

As I always wanted to bring alumni with career stories to the classroom, I reached out to many over the years and asked if they wouldn't mind sharing with our students. As it turned out, no one ever said that they could not do it and in fact, many found that they truly enjoyed the experience. One of those being **Dan Bane**, the CEO of Trader Joe's, who came to class wearing his uniform Hawaiian shirt and name badge that said "Team Member Dan." He had played on a USC national collegiate championship baseball team and then started his career as an accountant before moving up to his current position.

He told the following story to the students: When he was working in one of the stores during his periodic store visits, he carried a customer's bags to the car. I interrupted him, to be sure the students saw the significance of what he was telling them. It became obvious to them that nothing is more important for ANY employee of a company than taking care of the customer.

Finishing the story—the woman he had helped reached into her purse to give him a tip, to which he told her that it wasn't necessary—the Trader Joe's employees didn't accept gratuities. She then offered some career advice to him: "You seem like a nice young man, so I hope you have more ambition than just to be a bag boy at Trader Joe's!" He thanked her and returned to the store. She never knew what he did for the company.

My visit to the offices of **Scott Boras**, one of sport's most successful agents, was a true delight. The baseball memorabilia that he collected over the years represented a trip down memory lane for any fan. It also was easy to see how he was so successful in his career. He and his team of assistants have collected more baseball stats—a statistics-driven business in the first place—than anyone. This has helped him over the years to command the highest compensation for his clients.

For example, in his "war room" one can quickly see on the screen the difference in performance between a Hall of Fame baseball player from the sixties and a current one, or even between two current ones. That comparison gives Scott the ammunition he needs to present the best case for his clients during the contract renegotiation process. As he has said, he has more data than any of the major-league baseball teams he negotiates with, which gives him the advantage of representing clients.

I have had the privilege to sit with Scott at numerous major-league baseball games, and I love hearing him analyze the players, their skills, and their opportunities. All of his knowledge is driven by his understanding of their individual statistics, and his success depends on his being able to deliver that message to the various teams on behalf of his player-clients.

In 1985, I joined the American Porsche Design as its president, and I reported to CEO **Sam Tucker**, who had been a senior executive with Volkswagen of America. As we ran an international business owned by the Porsche family of Austria, Sam taught me how to deal with a global business environment. I brought the marketing and retail skills to the business, but he brought the skill set to deal with a different approach than I might have seen.

I learned a great deal with Austrian ownership, advertising firms, product development, and banking operations. The American way of doing business is not always best, and we need to keep an open mind to alternative ways. Our Porsche brand name was the fourth strongest in the world at the time, so we had that on our side, but we still needed product placement with retailers.

I was comfortable ultimately opening our own store to highlight all of our products, so when I became the CEO, I made it happen. I am not sure telling our owners AFTER having signed the store's lease was a good idea, but fortunately Sam supported me taking the calculated risk and it worked. Business increased with all our accounts as consumers could see the breadth of the line in our store, even if they opted to buy it at their favorite store.

As I ventured into the entrepreneurial world, one of my first experiences brought me a partner, who truly taught me a lot. **Dale Kelley** was the banker on the first company we bought. As he operated from that vantage point, you could see that he really wanted to be an owner, rather than a financing banker. So, when the next acquisition opportunity came down the road, he asked if he could join my company in ownership, as he would leave his position to do so. He was a competitive guy, an African American who held the record basketball season scoring average for Northwestern University for a number of years and who transferred his athletic skills to the business world smoothly.

As a partner, Dale was creative, curious, and communicative—great traits of a partner—and he approached it all withs LOTS of optimism. He had a strong moral code as well. After we sold the business, he took his personality, his values, and his optimism and he became a minister. I watched him change his careers twice, from banker to entrepreneur and from entrepreneur to pastor—and he was great in all three of those callings.

Career advice that I often shared with Marshall graduates and that my father-in-law once shared with me: Find a company that will get you into the Young Presidents' Organization. I suppose I can broaden that by suggesting that you find organizations outside your place of employment that will offer unbiased feedback, supportive encouragement, and networking opportunities. There are many out there: Vistage, Entrepreneurs' Organization, Young Entrepreneur Council, Business Network International, and Family Business Network, to name a few. Throughout my career, membership in YPO has been an invaluable resource.

The group was started back in 1951 by **Ray Hickok**, whose father had founded the Hickok Belt Company. When Ray was just twenty-nine, his father passed away and he took over the company. He had no idea how to be president of a company, and so he decided to reach out to other guys who were on the younger side and who were running companies to see if they would talk to him and share advice. As it turns out, once these presidents were sure that they weren't talking to a competitor, they had plenty to say. In fact, they were eager to share their experiences with another president, because nobody but another president could really understand the position, the stakes, and the decision-making processes involved in running a company. That's how YPO started.

Today there are over thirty thousand members worldwide, and the criteria to join is that you have to be president of your company or the publisher or managing partner—whatever the top leadership title is in your industry—and the company needs to meet some minimum sales revenue and minimum number of employee requirements—you can't be a one-man operation. As for the "Young" part of it, you have to join prior to the age of forty-five, and at fifty you get booted into the older "alum" group—they now call it "Gold." As a member you attend monthly chapter meetings with the entire group in your area, and once a month you also meet with a smaller forum group of ten or twelve members.

What gets said in those forums never gets repeated outside the forums. You're in a completely confidential setting in which you can discuss things that affect your work life in a personal way—a child with alcohol use disorder, problems with a spouse, an illness, and interoffice affairs. The members of a forum can function as one another's private board of advisors and be very open and honest about what they think should or shouldn't be done about any given situation.

**Questions About Your Career:**

- Are you moving in a direction where you see progress and are happy with it?
- Are you maximizing the time you are in that company and that position, learning as much as you can?
- Are you aware of what other employees and departments do at your place of work?
- Are you asking as many questions as you can about the business so you can build your learning of it?
- What would your ideal workplace environment look like?

Steve Ballmer (second from left) and friend Wally Walker (right)—Seattle buddies.

Elon Musk and a graduating student, Wendy.

President William J. Clinton.

President George W. Bush and Mrs. Laura Bush.

Evan Spiegel, CEO of Snap.

Serial entrepreneur
Richard Rosenblatt.

Venture capitalist Tim Draper.
© 2018 UNIVERSITY OF SOUTHERN CALIFORNIA (PHOTO BY WILLIAM VASTA)

Friend Mark McKinley and Coach Pete Carroll.

Mervyn's founder Merv Morris proud of graduating grandson Ryan.

Congressional Medal of Honor winner Walter Ehlers at Normandy.

Queen Rania of Jordan at The Greenbrier.

Margaret Spellings and our close friends Bill Baribault and Clark Hooper.

USC President Max Nikias with wonderful benefactors Frank and Jill Fertitta.

Big wave surfer Laird Hamilton and US ambassador Thomas J. Barrack Jr.

Nancy and Greg Hillgren—family is EVERYTHING.

Great supporter Lloyd Greif with Gloria Steinem.

Investor Alex Cappello (second from left).

Romance "expert" Debbie Williams and husband Jim, my fraternity brother.

Honorary consul of Monaco and former roommate Thomas E. Horn.

Former Secretary of State Henry A. Kissinger.

Graduating student Sophia Doyle.

# Chapter 6

# Preparation and Perseverance

Academic careers, business careers, and life in general rarely unfold in a pure linear fashion. There are digressions and complications, and even if you might plan to go from point A to point B, the path there might not be a straight line.

So, part of being smart about preparation is to be prepared to be unprepared. I've already spoken about the value of an MBA, but that degree does not prepare you to step into a business career the way that training at a trade school might prepare you to start working on HVAC units. In fact, most entry-level jobs in the corporate world are going to require a lot of on-the-job training, no matter where you get your MBA. Having earned that degree simply allows you to stand a little straighter and have confidence that you can compete in an arena where you find yourself working.

**William Jefferson Clinton** and **George W. Bush** were the most impressive masters of "unprepared" preparedness I had ever seen. I recall President Clinton and me preparing to take the stage together at an event in Beverly Hills—a Q&A session for the Association for Corporate Governance. I was to be the moderator and he was to give the perspectives of his presidential experience with freedom to answer any way he liked. I was introduced to Clinton in the "greenroom" and exchanged some cordial pleasantries, but what really struck me was how absorbed he was in the presentation being made onstage before our session—a talk from a brilliant cancer researcher that we could watch on a closed-circuit television. We waited to go out onstage until he had the chance to see the entire presentation. I could almost hear the gears of Mr. Clinton's ferociously curious mind turning as he followed the researcher's every word.

Then, it was time for us to take the stage. As per his office's request, I had submitted five questions to be asked of him, and I started out our discussion by asking him the first of those. He answered the question coolly and confidently. But he felt his answer needed some historical context and he established that by going back to the Middle Ages. As he carefully moved forward through history, I began to worry that I might not ever get to a second question in our allotted hour. Just as my worry started to edge near panic, dang if he didn't stick the landing and wrap up with a conclusion that, despite the professorial lead-in, was brilliant and insightful. I was worried that he was circling the airport so long that he might not get the plane to land.

I did in fact get to all five questions and as we finished the hour, I mentioned the fact that there were rumors flying about his wife possibly running for president as well. He answered by saying that it was her decision and her decision alone and that she would make it at the appropriate time. Then he added, "I have always said she is the smartest person I have ever met, and I know she will do a great job," and he began to tear up. Many people have heard about his emotional side, but I was seeing it up close and personal—and wasn't quite sure how to respond to it. It didn't seem right to push him any harder on a subject that clearly stirred some raw feelings, so I simply said, "Thank you, Mr. President, for being here with us today, for what you have done for our country and God bless America." We stood up together to acknowledge the standing ovation and he learned over to me.

"You bailed me out," he said, "I was losing it."

I responded, "Yeah and I didn't have any Kleenex!"

Not too long after that event, I had a chance to interview President Clinton a second time on the USC campus. He started off by saying, "I told Jim that after our last time together, I would work hard to keep it together and give short answers."

He accomplished the former, but not the latter. We talked a lot about current events and how the ultimate outcomes of situations on the news might impact our society. His answers were never what one would call "short" by any stretch, but they were always compelling. His knowledge about so many subjects was truly impressive. I don't think I've ever met anyone who was such a natural consummate learner or anyone who took such evident great pleasure in sharing what he had learned.

My first interview with former President George W. Bush also took place in Beverly Hills at the same Association for Corporate Governance event, different year. My rules for this interview as established by President Bush's office were to submit five questions beforehand and be sure to end the interview on time. They also did not want me to ask any questions about his predecessors in office, a sign of respect for fellow leaders.

As I waited outside the greenroom for him to finish with an appointment, I all of a sudden heard him bellow out "Ellis, get in here." (Little did I know this was an ingrained habit; he would never call me by my first name.) Apparently, he wanted me to bail him out of the meeting he was in and so as soon as I walked in, that other meeting was over.

Our conversation on the stage lasted exactly an hour as he requested and it proved to me, as well as the thirteen hundred people present, that this leader had complete control of the facts as they pertained to his time in office. Despite his reputation for being more detached about such details, he demonstrated an in-depth understanding of the foreign policy ramifications that grew from the decisions made around 9/11 and the fiscal monetary issues that came with the global financial crisis of 2007–2008. His presidency had had a lot of speed bumps and potholes, and he carefully walked us through them all.

At the end of our time, the president took the initiative to play moderator and asked me if any of the audience were my USC donors. When I told him that a good percentage of them were UCLA alums, he spoke directly to the crowd and exhorted them to give me money.

"He's a dean—they raise money. You have to help him," said Mr. Bush.

There was no sudden rush to write checks to the school, but I appreciated the president's effort on my behalf. And I loved the fact that he was comfortable enough in that setting to let his great sense of humor shine through.

As we walked off the stage, I told him my youngest son was in the audience and asked if I could invite him backstage. President Bush had no problem with that, and when I brought Rob back, the president asked him, "So Rob, what are you doing now?" Rob, a recent USC graduate, answered quickly, "I am the same as you, Mr. President—I am unemployed," which brought great laughter from all. With that, Mr. Bush put his arm around Rob and said, "Let's go have our picture taken together," and off they walked.

As with President Clinton, my second interview with President Bush was at USC, and this time he was joined by his former First Lady, Mrs. Laura Bush. Prior to the event, people gathered in the office of the president of the university to meet with the Bushes. I was elsewhere but summoned to the office with the words "Mr. Bush wants to see Ellis." As Gail and I walked into the room, I heard a familiar bellow: "Ellis, get over here." I sensed that everyone in the office was shocked and wondering, "How does 'Ellis' know President Bush?"

Onstage for our event, the repartee between the Bushes and myself was terrific and genuine. We talked a great deal about Laura's initiatives to aid women from developing countries. Mindful of how adeptly Mr. Bush had handled the detailed questions I'd asked him at our previous event, I grilled him once more about the financial crisis, the 9/11 issues, the Asian financial meltdown, and a few more heavy topics. Finally, he stopped me mid-query by asking, "Ellis, I thought you were going to ask me easy questions, like 'What's your favorite color?'" To which I quickly responded, "Mr. President, this is USC, not Yale."

He put on a very stern face and said, "I am the one who is supposed to make the jokes." Laura gracefully got us back on track for a few more serious exchanges, and we ended by talking a bit about the president's new passion for painting.

Becoming successful requires time and energy—exactly what an MBA requires—and therefore, earning a degree is smart preparation for your future. I came out of grad school knowing that I would rarely be the smartest guy in the room but that I could outwork just about anybody. When I stepped up to the dean's position, I began to think about how I might be prepared for the issues and challenges I would encounter in that role, and the answer was not to start putting a doctoral thesis together. Instead, I made sure that I had positions on boards of directors for various commercial and nonprofit entities. By serving on boards, I could really keep my toe in the water of business culture and have an ongoing sense of the practical aspects of business. I didn't want Marshall to be an academic environment in which people got caught up in the theory side of business. What I wanted to do was marry the theory and the practical sides of business; it was just as important to bring practitioners into the classroom as it was to have great professors, and because I was out there sitting on boards, I always felt well prepared to bring the academic and business worlds together.

Preparation is what gets you ready to do a great job. Perseverance is what you need to see a job through to completion. One of the saddest encounters in life is in meeting someone who could not finish a path they started on. Life is certainly open to exploration—if you take a few steps down a particular path to see if you want to go that way—and realize that you don't—then not completing what you set out on is a valid option. But if you start something with the express purpose of completing the task, then you need to be sure you do so. Each time you leave an achievable goal unachieved, it becomes easier to give up the next time you're faced with a challenge.

Especially in the business world, no matter how small an assignment is, the point of taking it on is seeing it to the end. Leaders finish what they start. It is as simple as that.

Is it ever too late to finish what you've started? Perhaps, in some situations there is a point of no-return-on-investment at which pursuit of a goal is no longer worth it. However, most of us are never as close to that point as we think we are. In fact, sometimes the successes that take the longest to achieve are the sweetest.

My professor at Harvard Business School for the Planning in the Business Environment course was **Ram Charan**, who has since gained fame as the author of some twenty-five books on corporate leadership—boards and CEOs to be specific—and is a renowned consultant to corporations. He was the first professor we encountered on our first day at HBS and began his class announcing, “Ladies and gentlemen, welcome to Harvard.” That was the extent of Professor Charan’s orientation. Then he said, “Mr. Frederick, would you start the first case on Alcoa.” That immediately grabbed our attention—I know he scared the hell out of me, though I was quite relieved not to be my classmate, young Ken Frederick.

Ram taught us a lot, but the one thing that has stayed with me for all these years is his advice to spend 10 percent of your time reading—not just about your business, but about the world. For years, I subscribed to over fifty periodicals of all sorts of topics, just to continue learning. Great preparation.

Ram continues to work with CEOs around the world, coaching them on strategy for their firms. He truly lives out of his suitcase being on the road ALL the time. He opened an office in Texas but for years has never been there. He lives with change and is the embodiment of it.

If you can develop a sense of where the world is going, you can be ready to move when it moves. I was amazed at how many companies were able to stay nicely afloat during the recent pandemic because they were ready with contingency plans—staffwise, financially, and strategically. It was a result of great preparation—the kind of informed readiness that Professor Charan would advise to any of us.

Students would come to my office on a regular basis just to talk for five minutes or so—many would say it was intimidating to spend any more time than that in the dean’s office! One, however, who came in to see me in 2007 had quite an influence on me with a great lesson:

He walked in and said, “Hi, I am **Larsen Jensen**, and I was told to come and meet you.” I responded, “Hi Larsen, are you a business school student?” He replied in the negative, but I had him come to take a seat in the office anyway and asked, "Larsen, do you have any goals in life?"

"Yes sir, I have three—I want to win a gold medal in the Olympic Games, be a United States Navy SEAL, and be a United States senator!" He was pretty firm about this, so once I picked myself up off the floor, I asked him if he was prepared to actually do any of these. Yes, he said—not only was he a competitive swimmer, but he had won a silver medal in the previous Athens games. That's why he felt he could win gold in Beijing.

He fell a little short of his swimming goal—he won the bronze medal in Beijing. But he made the podium for the second time in his life, which only VERY few do. When the Olympic team went to Washington, DC, to meet the president, he took his dad—one of the nicest things that a dad can experience, I would guess, is to have his son take him to the Oval Office.

Larsen served for seven years in the United States Navy as a SEAL and was deployed a number of times to Iraq and Afghanistan. When he came in to see me after his tours of duty, he was planning on leaving the navy to go to graduate school. I asked him how it was being overseas. His response was: "We leave SO much over there in the way of tanks, equipment, supplies—it's just such a waste of taxpayer money."

"That's great, Larsen." He looked at me quizzically and asked why I said that.

To which I responded, "You are already thinking like a United States senator."

"You never have forgotten that, have you?" he asked. And I had not.

His goals are lofty, but he is two-thirds of the way there.

Larsen graduated from the Graduate School of Business at Stanford and has gone into the venture capital business. He is a happy husband and a wonderful father. I have never worried about whether he will be a success in life. He has not held elective office yet, but keep an eye out for him. He still holds the American record in the four-hundred-meter freestyle, so winning is in his blood.

When I asked **Evan Spiegel** to be a commencement speaker after having been introduced by a mutual friend, he was a bit reluctant, given that he had gone to Stanford but had not graduated. He was a cofounder of Snapchat (now Snap) as a student and then, at twenty-four, was worried that he had nothing to impart to graduating students who were maybe two or three years younger than him. I assured him that he had much to talk about and was happy when he agreed to do it.

As the time came for him to speak, I put my hand on his arm and asked if he was ready. He said yes, but the shaking in his arm told me that he was apprehensive, as many in that situation often are. I said, "Well, it's showtime," and introduced him.

Evan stood up to the podium, looked out at some one thousand graduates and five thousand families and friends, took a deep breath, and said, "This is SO cool." They exploded in applause. He looked over to where his mother sat and said, "Mom, I told you I would make it to graduation," whereby the audience exploded again in applause.

He told of his journey up to a most recent moment where he had turned down an outright sale of the company for $3 billion to Facebook! He had a passion for his concept and his company and felt like there were great days ahead. The audience was with him every step of the way, and when he had finished, he sat down to rousing applause.

Whether it was due to what he saw and felt that day, which we even talked about privately, or another reason, some years later Evan returned to Stanford and finished his degree. He was a successful entrepreneur and he had married and become a dad, but completing his studies at Stanford was obviously something that was very satisfying for him.

**It feels better to finish than to walk away.**

Throughout my career as a dean, there have been several times when I've been asked to assist a student in completing their degree. In some ways the university is meant to be an oasis apart from the struggles and challenges of the "real" world, but that doesn't always protect a student from real-world difficulties. Unstable home lives, financial crises, mental health issues—there are many complications that can throw a student off track in their pursuit of a degree.

Considering how hard it is to get into a top university and how much emphasis is put on the value of a college degree in about any career path these days, it's not surprising that someone who begins college-level studies but can't complete them ends up feeling devastated. Self-confidence and self-worth are undermined, and I've seen departing students who seem to be doing all they can to conceal the emptiness they feel as if there were now a hole in their heart. So, when I've had the opportunity to assist a student in finding some creative way to work toward their degree, I've always been very happy to do so.

One of most creative—and longest—paths to a degree was taken by a student named **Robert Shotwell**. Bob's USC undergrad career was cut short by a larger-than-usual real-world problem—namely, War World II. He was one semester shy of graduating in 1943 when he was inducted into the US Army and joined the Corps of Engineers. After four years of service, Bob was a married man with a family to support and bills to pay; the thought of becoming a student again seemed impractical at best. Instead, Shotwell embarked on a marketing career in the emerging information industry. He had an extremely successful career with the Olivetti Underwood corporation and went on to found Robert Shotwell and Associates, an independent consulting and marketing firm that advised entrepreneurs.

At that point, the moral of Shotwell's story might have been: "You don't need to finish what you start, because you can do pretty darn well without a college degree."

But that lack of degree bothered Bob—in no small part because he'd been so close to achieving something that he really wanted to achieve. And he didn't want just any bachelor's degree from any school. He wanted what he had originally aimed for—a USC business degree.

So, at the age of eighty-one, Bob sent me a letter asking if I might be able to facilitate the completion of his studies at the Marshall School. I was very excited about helping with his challenge.

The first obstacle was geography. He lived in Maine, so taking classes on campus was not going to be a possibility. My team and I collaborated closely with him to find universities close to his home where he could take courses and have credits transferred to USC. It took us a few more years to make it happen, but we finally figured out how to help him properly earn his degree.

As graduation day grew closer, I spoke with Bob and added a stipulation to his credit requirements: If at all possible, I wanted him to come to Los Angeles and be physically present for the graduation ceremonies.

He made it and was even prouder to have done it the same year that his granddaughter would be graduating from Marshall. He looked great in a cap and gown—with a huge smile across his face. When his name was announced at the ceremonies, he was introduced as "the oldest graduate in the history of the USC Marshall School of Business." His classmates—all a good sixty years younger than him—erupted into a long, LONG, heartfelt standing ovation. At eighty-five, Bob walked across that stage with all the pride and joy that had been denied him decades before.

His USC career didn't quite end there. A couple of years later, Bob was in touch with me and let me know that he was coming back to Los Angeles for a week. He wondered if he might be able to sit in on some classes while he was here. Of course!

Not long after that, on an otherwise ordinary Thursday, I was excited to see Bob crossing Figueroa Street, walking toward campus with a Starbucks coffee in his hand and a sizable backpack over his shoulder. I stopped to talk to him, thinking that he would just be happy to see me. But my "Hello Bob!" was met with a very curt response: "Jim, I don't have time to talk now—I'm late for class."

He made a tremendous impression on his professors and classmates that week. And the time spent at USC wasn't the last challenge he set for himself. He traveled widely (with a license plate that read "Go RVs"). In 2013, he drove his Mini Cooper the entire length of the fabled Route 66, and the following year he drove a round trip from Maine to Florida to explore historic hotels along the way. And—oh, yes—he also took up bungee jumping. He died in 2018 at the age of ninety-seven, a beloved elder in his community and a mentor to several generations of "youngsters."

Robert Shotwell didn't really "need" a USC degree to make his life relevant and significant. But the fact that he wanted to finish what he started points to the perseverance and enthusiasm that he brought to everything in his life. Walking away from a goal we could have achieved diminishes us and makes the next goal much harder to achieve. Achieving a goal we set out for—even when a world war and a sixty-year hiatus gets in the way—results in rewards that are even bigger than the goal itself.

During my early years in the Young Presidents' Organization, I met **Alex Cappello**, who became a lifelong friend. Alex is an investment banker who has experienced almost as many business low points as he has high points. In speaking to students, he would tell the story of how at one time in his life he was as much as $30 million in debt but managed to get out of it all without declaring bankruptcy. Here is a man with complete optimism in life, which he embodied both as a college yell leader and a track star.

He later began to experience difficult physical issues that ultimately resulted in him using a wheelchair for much of the day, but one never knew it when talking to him on the phone. If you just went by the energy and positive attitude of his voice, Alex was still the vibrant runner of his youth, working tirelessly to help his family, his friends, and his clients. He had persevered not just to finish something left undone, but also to continue an active life in the face of tremendous obstacles. He remains one of the favorite speakers of my students for the stories that conveyed going to the depths and pulling oneself out of them.

**Sabrina Kay** is not only a great example of perseverance, but she is also the embodiment of the American dream. She came to the United States at the age of nine from her native Korea, and since the day she set foot on American soil, she has not stopped moving forward. She has had her share of hurdles; for example, she didn't speak a word of English so she had to learn a new language, and early on in her adulthood, she became a single mom. But she has consistently jumped the hurdles she's faced with style. She did her undergraduate college work in computer science and applied that learning to computer-aided design and manufacturing in the fashion industry, ultimately building a fashion institute. A true believer in education, she followed that success by going back to school to earn her MBA, a master's in education, and from the University of Pennsylvania, a doctorate in work-based learning.

As she moved through her years in Southern California, Sabrina founded businesses, bought businesses, and advised other young entrepreneurs. She founded a graduate-level institution, Fremont College, and has used it to help educate inner-city youth about ways they can successfully launch their own careers. She has never forgotten the struggles of her own early years and wants to help others deal with the struggles they may face.

I have watched her over the years generate accomplishments and garner recognition through her hard work and am always amazed at what she can get done. She connects people in so many ways and is exemplary in her networking skills. All of this started with a difficult beginning, but she never gave up on trying to be successful in this country. She was determined to make a difference and she is doing just that.

If there were a trophy for perseverance, I might have to give it to **Cornelius Shields**. He has worked on his "start-up" business for nearly twenty years and is finally starting to see his hard work pay off. "Corny" came from an established East Coast family (that even has a sailboat class named after it) but left for the west after a successful career on Wall Street and journeyed to California. Full of ideas, and ideals, Corny thought about birthing an innovation that could shape the future of sustainable energy for many years to come. He devised a way to turn organic waste into carbon-negative fuel—namely, "UltraGreen" hydrogen. It is the ultimate full circle of life where one's waste becomes another's fuel.

In 2008, the technology that Shields developed was given an on-site pilot test with the Los Angeles County Sanitation District. The test was successful enough that Corny's company, KORE, was able to build prototypes of units that could turn the city's organic waste into biogas. Today, KORE has developed a large-scale commercial facility that produces renewable hydrogen for its clients.

A few years ago, he and his wife welcomed their first child, giving Corny even greater stakes in the future. He has been "living his business" for many years now, and it is a credit to his vision that he has had the ability to stay with a project that will ultimately benefit so many other people and so many other companies. In his drive to leave his son a better world, Corny's perseverance is unparalleled.

A former student of mine, **Chris Botsford**, never let anything get in the way of achieving his goals. Chris came to USC having played varsity soccer in high school, but he really thought he wanted to play collegiate golf, an athletic switch that definitely caught my attention. He worked very hard at golf during his undergraduate years and was named the team cocaptain in his senior year. Pretty amazing for a young man everyone thought was a soccer player. But Chris was not done. As a fifth-year senior, Chris played in the Western Amateur Golf Championship and won it. For a player who was a walk-on to his college team to be named team captain was quite an accomplishment. But again, Chris was not done.

He raised funds from family and friends to give him the financial support he needed to take a shot at becoming a professional golfer, a very difficult undertaking. After his amateur successes, Chris wanted to see what he could do against the very best in his sport. While he did not make it for long on the professional circuit, he gave it his best effort. If he hadn't, he might well have spent the rest of his life wondering about what might have been. When he finished his short career in golf, he sent thank-you notes to his financial sponsors and paid them back whatever he could. Chris's golf career didn't end the way he wanted, but his perseverance gave him a sense of achievement he carried with him for the rest of his life.

**Questions About Preparation and Perseverance:**

- Do you know what track in life you are preparing for and how to do it best?
- What could you do to prepare for success in the job you want?
- Do you have a track record of staying with your goals or giving up on them early?

# Chapter 7

# Don't Sell Sales Short

Some of the best ways to start one's career after college are working for an accounting firm, being an analyst with an investment banking firm, or, for those not comfortable with numbers yet, working in sales. The concept of sales has always been negative, as in that of a used car salesman, a door-to-door peddler, or an insurance salesperson. And yet, EVERY day of our business careers, we are selling, with the top salesperson being the CEO of the company.

Students are selling when they are trying to get into a particular university, when they are trying to get a date with someone they are attracted to, or when they are trying to join a club or organization. We are ALWAYS selling. Good salespeople are everywhere and can be huge successes everywhere. There is nothing negative about selling, but rather the manner in which it is done.

Good salespeople are storytellers. As I was raising funds for various projects and visions at the Marshall School of Business, I was selling those visions by telling stories. I was not walking around with my hand out asking for money. I told the story that I truly believed in and hoped something hit a positive nerve with them enough to make a gift to the school.

Some great storytellers who have crossed my path warrant your hearing about them. **Harvey Mackay** was the CEO of an envelope company in Minneapolis when I first met him. He had the innate ability to tell stories with the best of them, but more importantly, he knew how to transform those stories into revenue for his company, and then into revenue for himself personally.

As successful as Harvey was in selling envelopes—and he had some wonderful techniques for doing so—he became more successful when he put his thoughts and experiences down on the page and became one of America's most inspirational authors and speakers. He has written seven *New York Times* bestseller books including the highly influential ***Swim with the Sharks Without Being Eaten Alive***. He has spoken all over the world and has leveraged his success into a great deal of philanthropic work.

Harvey's strength was in knowing everything about his customers that he possibly could know, and keeping records of that information so he could use it over and over. He made things personal with customers as much as he could, to endear himself to them. Envelopes are a commodity, but Harvey made them special by the way he treated his customers.

Harvey is an incredibly friendly guy and one of the ultimate networkers in this world—so much so that I am not entirely sure how we met, but I am honored to be a part of his network.

His goodwill and positive spirit made him a lifesaver for me. About two weeks prior to graduation one year, the planned commencement speaker for the MBA graduates at USC Marshall inexplicably bailed on me, and I was left holding the bag. Harvey had been kind enough to send me copies of his books, so I knew he would have plenty to say. On a whim, I called him and asked if he might be able to take this speaking gig. Without hesitation, he agreed.

He flew on his own plane to Los Angeles and delivered an address that was eloquent, memorable, and inspiring.

An imbalance in our friendship, however, arose a few years later. I was sitting next to him at dinner one night when it occurred to me that he had stopped talking, which salesmen, and particularly Harvey, never do. When I looked over at him, he was pointing to his throat. Before I could figure out what to do, his wife Carol Ann, seated on the other side of me, reacted with speed. She jumped up behind him and gave him the Heimlich maneuver—propelling a problematic piece of chicken across the room. I had the opportunity to be a literal lifesaver and I blew it. Sorry, Harvey, and thank you, Carol Ann.

Everyone says car people are born to sell—they truly are always selling. **Roy Roberts** is no exception. He rose up the ranks of General Motors to be the highest-ranking African American in the industry, and only the second to ever be at such a level. It was easy to see why: He had personality, intelligence, and tremendous strength of character. I was able to see his leadership skills (which could easily translate to salesmanship skills) one day as we walked the assembly line of a General Motors plant. Roy knew their names, including those of family members, and something about each of the workers on the line. It was amazing to watch him walk down the line, asking about the son/daughter/spouse of a worker—and it was real, not rehearsed. He cared enough about his employees to put in the effort to make these personal connections.

Roy knew what it took to sell a product, a concept, a system—he could lead, and he could sell. Once he left the automotive industry, he became president of the Boy Scouts of America, and did great work supporting the city of Detroit. He is a giving guy, which came back to him in so many ways, as it would if he were selling cars on the floor of a dealership. The personal touch is so important in selling.

For my first semester as a professor, I was asked to teach a course in sales management. The previous semester that class only had eighteen students, and if that continued, the course would be canceled. True academics don't like to teach such a class, as it rarely ties into their research subjects—and that was why they asked me to teach it.

I felt that the right way for students to learn sales was to hear stories from the front—from those who had been on the sales "battlefield." One of the first to speak to the class was **Craig Tschudi**, who sold custom apparel to executives by coming to their offices and fitting them there.

Craig was calm, addressing objections in a positive manner. Everything he did was positive—nothing negative. He was soft spoken, with a Texas accent, and was never overbearing nor pushy. Just told the story of the clothing and how he let customers make up their own mind. The students were relatively unimpressed, until one of them asked how much money he could make—when he answered with the figure, they mobbed him after class!!

**Rick Whipple**, **Chuck Akers**, and **Bill Spooner** were salesmen to my department as I worked as a buyer for The Broadway department stores—in various departments as Housewares, Men's Sportswear, and Young Men's/Boys. They told their stories in numbers. Data was their friend. Sales by SKU, by store, by size, by color—all they had to do was show us the results and we would reorder into the remaining inventory. They had told the story originally, which caused the item to be sent into our forty-five stores, but they then generated reorders with their numbers. This is where comfort with numbers, and data analysis, helps in sales. They were successful in their careers—they made me a success in return.

One incident I remember well is when I was a housewares buyer; **Bernie Abramson** came in to see me with a new cooking timer that he wanted me to buy. I asked him if by any chance he had been in one of our stores recently, to which he honestly said no. Then I had to tell him that we were already buying that item, and it was selling in our stores! This shows how truly important it is to do your research prior to trying to close a deal—he embarrassed himself by not looking at our assorted items in the store, where he would have seen that it would be unwise to show us something we already had. Know your customer.

Another way to get to know your customer was exhibited by **Elmer Fredericks**, who sold me his apparel distribution company back in the early 1980s. He was a true road warrior, driving from customer to customer around the western United States, for eleven months of the year. He kept personal records of all his customers—their names, birthdays, anniversaries, spouses' and children's names/birthdays—and sent cards and notes to them all the time. They felt a personal connection to him and would always give him the benefit of the doubt when he was selling to them.

If understanding the customer is crucial to one's success in selling, **Rob Rodin**, the former CEO of Marshall Industries, made it sound simple. His book ***Free, Perfect, and Now*** really says as succinctly as possible how the customer wants their products or services. To achieve success, we have to work toward those goals—give it to them at the best possible price, in the best quality, and as soon as possible. Rob worked hard to satisfy his customers with that mantra in mind and built a spectacular business in doing so.

All the previous examples of successful sales concepts, if properly implemented, can make the role of a salesperson easier. The job is not to just get an order and be done with the customer, but to understand them, to tell the story to them so they identify with your offering, and then to follow up with them long after the deal has been made.

There is a great deal of opportunity to use artificial intelligence in identifying and qualifying sales prospects, but the story and the sale must be accomplished by an individual. AI will not replace the sales force, but merely give it more weapons with which to attack the appropriate market.

**Questions About Sales:**

- Are you confident in your ability to tell a story? Can you practice that?
- Think of the instances in your life where you sold something, including yourself. Did it go well? Could it have gone better? How?
- How can you improve your storytelling, hence your sales ability? Do you need to do it?

## Chapter 8

# Risk Management and Disappointment

It is often said that anybody who's an entrepreneur is a risk-taker. That's not entirely true. Good entrepreneurs evaluate the landscape and assess the situation around them and then make the decision to move or not. So, the key to their success isn't simply the act of taking a risk—it's in their ability to spot opportunities after having processed as much information as is available to them. There will always be a lack of certain information and some unexpected contingencies, but if you've got a feel for what you're doing, you know when you've got enough information to justify the move you want to make. I always felt that was true when I was in the role of an entrepreneur, and I enjoyed the chess game of thinking entrepreneurially. Chess is a game you can learn and get better at. On the other hand, if you're always just rolling dice, you're counting directly on luck—and taking a bigger risk than you probably should.

Risk management isn't just the concern of entrepreneurs, though. It can be a part of almost any work you do. My first job as a buyer in a department store chain forced me to take risks because at times a buyer has to buy something they believe the customer wants before the customer knows they want it. All data points to "green" being next season's color and you stock up on everything green and then the customers look at it and say,

"What's all this? We want blue." I remember buying things that would just not sell—the stuff would be sitting in the store, and I'd be thinking, "These customers are stupid—don't they know this is the hot new trend?" Well, if they don't want it, I'm the one who's stupid for misreading those trends. I had to learn when it was wise to take a risk and when I just had to mark everything down, get rid of it, and move on.

I learned how to find the balance of risk-taking and informed decision-making while working in the retail world. As a buyer, if you didn't take a risk, you might be making a mistake because you could be losing the chance to get ahead of everyone else and do something that would distinguish you from your competition. If you wait until a risk feels like a safe bet—that usually means the competition already has it.

A strange example of all of this occurred in 1975 when a buyer from another department came to see me and asked if I would take a look at a new product. He didn't understand it and wanted my thoughts. I went to his office and looked at what he was being pitched. It was a ROCK! A small, smooth rock with a little bit of straw in a small version of a box you might carry a pet in—a pet rock. It was obviously a gag, but the more I thought about it, the more I considered that people were feeling that the world was really a mess at the time, and maybe we needed something whimsical to bring a smile to our faces. A "pet rock" might just be the perfect whimsical thing for the moment. We agreed that he should buy a few and see what happened. Well, the trend took off out of nowhere, and that Christmas the number one selling gift item in the US was the pet rock. Betting on a $15 rock was a risk, especially since the guy producing them didn't even have a supply chain—the rocks were being picked up off the beach in Rosarito, Mexico. But if that buyer didn't take the risk, he would not have had as strong a level of Christmas sales as he did, and if he had waited until this item was not a risk, because it was such a hot trend, he would have missed out completely. The pet rock fad only lasted about six months, so if he had waited to have his order processed, he would have been stuck with a whole kennel full of unsellable rocks.

I also remember when a new way to make coffee at home came along: Instead of the percolator that most people had used before, here was a drip coffee maker called Mr. Coffee (the brand used Yankee great Joe DiMaggio as a pitchman). I remember buying a few for our stores without much conviction that it would be a hit, but the day that I saw the May Co.—my competition—run an ad for it, my boss came to me and asked why we didn't have more in our stores already. That was my fault for not taking the risk when I should have seen it was the smart thing to do. There's risk and there's timing, and good timing helps mitigate the risk. You've got the right price, going up against the right competition—that's all part of timing. You have to be able to make a bold decision. If you wait until that decision would be obvious to anyone, you're not an entrepreneur, you're a follower of the market. Money can be made that way too, but the real money and the excitement and the satisfaction are in knowing how and when to take a risk.

At USC, one of the big risks we took was in creating a Master of Business program for veterans, which we talked about earlier. It felt good to offer that opportunity to service members, but we hoped they had an interest in coming to it even though we didn't truly know how successful a program like that would be. It turned out to be a gigantic success, and it differentiated USC from other schools. That was a risk in the academic setting that paid off.

When you take a risk in investing, you do as much research as you possibly can on the companies you're investing in; then you take the plunge and buy the stock. That approach would extend to taking a job—don't take positions unless you've done as much research as you can on what the job entails and what is going to be expected of you in that role. The more informed you are, the more you're reducing the risk. Risk can also be mitigated by trust if you know people who work there, are referred there, or even know the person hiring you.

There's always an element of risk in partnerships, whether it's business partnerships or life partnerships. That risk can't always be mitigated by research because at some point, the way people are going to behave or react to shifting circumstances can't be quantified in data you can analyze. Human behavior can sometimes be predictable, but it can also be a wild card, so the way partners interact and whether a partnership becomes mutually beneficial to both partners is a risk that can't always be mitigated. I've had partnerships that were terrible and partnerships that were pretty good. You can see what went right or wrong in retrospect, but going into those partnerships you had to rely a lot more on trust than on analytics.

In terms of personal risks, I have always thought you should start with "YES" and then work your way to "NO" if you have to, while evaluating the risks and rewards of saying yes. The key here is making sure you have the ability to trust. Trusting your gut feelings and trusting your friendships. It is important to be aware of how much risk is dependent on trust.

If you have a vision for what you want from your education, your career, your marriage, or any other aspect of your life, you are going to confront some risks in order to make that vision a reality. Vision is a sense of where you want to go. It helps you with your time management because if you have vision for who or where you want to be, it will override decisions that might lead you to spend some time with people you don't want to be around or do things you don't want to do. If things don't move you closer to your vision of what you want for yourself, you begin to avoid those things.

I had an assignment when I was a second-year student at business school: "Where will you be in forty years and how did you get there?" The assignment didn't use the word "vision," but really it was asking, "What is your vision for yourself?" I answered by dividing my future into four ten-year segments. I said I would spend the first ten years in the retail industry learning about customers and what they wanted. I would spend the next ten years in the manufacturing industry making what those customers wanted, and the third ten I would spend in government helping to make laws and policies that helped customers get goods and services they wanted. For the fourth ten years I said I'd be in business education, and forty years on, I would end up as dean of Harvard Business School. I started my life's journey and I got into the retail business—I was there for about thirteen years. Then I went into manufacturing for about ten years. I never got into government, but I got into education as I turned fifty—and wound up as dean of the Marshall School of Business.

The professor at Harvard had told us to put the paper away and not look at it again—to just see where we ended up. I found the paper about thirty-seven years after I'd written it. Within about a week of rereading it, I got a call from a classmate who said Harvard Business School was looking for a new dean and he wondered if I wanted him to recommend me. Just the fact that I could consider it floored me. My vision of myself as a twenty-three-year-old turned out to be accurate. For an additional *Twilight Zone* twist, the professor who assigned that essay was named Gordon Marshall. A different Gordon Marshall was the entrepreneur who gave the money to establish the Marshall School of Business at USC. I had been taught by Gordon Marshall in 1970 to work with Gordon Marshall in 2007.

From experience, you learn what works and that shapes your vision for your own future. However, the way we each build upon our experiences and the lessons we draw from them can differ greatly. I've developed quite a bit of respect for that difference. I've seen enough people succeed at taking a path I would have never considered that I've come to feel when someone tells you about their vision for themselves and it seems unrealistic or little bit off, you shouldn't ever say, "No, I tried that, and it didn't work." You just encourage someone to consider all the variables and possible obstacles. You don't want a vision to be a mirage—it should be something attainable. But you don't shy away from experiences that may become raw material to work with as you develop your decision-making process.

In taking risks necessary to pursue your vision, there's one more concept that comes into play: responsibility. Whatever you do—own it. Acknowledge your actions and—just as important—give somebody else credit for their accomplishments. If you did something that wasn't right, apologize right away and correct it. Accept the responsibility of being a boss or a supervisor, but make sure that credit goes to those who deserve it. Not allowing people to take credit for good work is the most unmotivating way to run a business. It sucks that spirit out of people. People don't necessarily need cash rewards for everything they do, but they want credit.

Here are a few examples of those who have taught me a great deal about risk, vision, and responsibility.

**Robert Liu** spent a fair amount of time on airplanes back in the 1970s. As a Chinese native who came to the United States to pursue his graduate studies at the University of Utah, all the while working for his family's passenger tire business in Taiwan, quite a bit of travel was necessary. Robert was working especially hard to advance the family business as there was still a great deal of resistance in the US to the concept of buying imported tires. All that time in the air gave him plenty of time to reflect upon where his life was headed, and one particular Pacific Southwest Airlines flight proved to be revelatory. He pondered how a small regional airline could stay alive, competing against the big companies and only charging slightly more than a Greyhound bus fare between Los Angeles and San Francisco. As the plane touched down on that flight, the tires squealed, causing Robert to think about something else he'd never considered before: Who made those tires? Was there enough profit to be made in such business niches as airplane tires?

That curiosity stuck with him, and in 1972 when he had finished school, Robert founded a US company called Tireco and began to distribute tires. His family background gave him expertise in automotive tires, but he expanded his vision and thinking to include ALL sorts of tires—from bicycle tires to those meant for golf carts, tractors, boat trailers, lawn mowers—even wheelbarrows. He hoped his expansive view of his products would help him capture markets that were relatively undeveloped. Some significant logistical problems had to be worked out. While Tireco's manufacturers in Taiwan were well acquainted with bicycle tires, the tires meant for golf carts, lawn mowers, and such had no market at the time, so manufacturers were producing something without quite understanding the end use of the product.

Robert put his vision and his strong entrepreneurship skills to bring all these different SKUs from another country to this one. Despite the obstacles, he persisted, and slowly but surely he convinced his partners to manufacture all the products he wanted to distribute in the US. However, once the tires were manufactured, Robert was confronted with another logistical problem. He wanted to be able to sell these various types of tires at a good price, but shipping them across the ocean added costs that American distributors couldn't cover. Tires are bulky and take up space in a shipping container, much of which is just air—yet no matter the air-to-rubber ratio you must pay for the entire container.

To help cut down on the costs of shipping, Robert figured out how to twist the uninflated tires into a configuration so that they almost fit inside one another. He was then able to put many more tires into a single container, for which he paid the same price, thereby lowering the cost of the individual tire. A brilliant operational move on his part.

Before long, his pioneering approach in the tire industry was steadily winning market share. Tireco has grown to be a force in the tire business, due to great entrepreneurial vision on the part of Robert Liu and his family. Even in a particular low-tech industry, there are many opportunities for change and improvement—it just takes a good thought process.

On a trip to the Middle East, I had the opportunity to have lunch with **Sheikh Saud bin Saqr Al Qasimi**, at the time the crown prince of the Emirate of Ras Al Khaimah. He later ascended to the role of ruler when his father passed away.

Saud, as he asked me to call him, had a vision for his tiny emirate of three hundred thousand people and set about to make it happen. RAK, as it is called, is the one emirate where oil has not been discovered, so it had to depend on very diverse industries for its economic success. Tourism was weak and he wanted to grow that. The largest industry was cement and industrial ceramics. He was looking to expand the knowledge and technology business in his country and set out to do so, even as his father was still the ruler.

The risk inherent in changing course for the country was that there would be unemployment and underutilization of assets, and any growth would be slow in the early years. He knew all that, but he also knew that he had no choice but for course correction.

He could not keep up with his "older brothers"—Abu Dhabi and Dubai—that were steeped in oil, so he had to go in a different direction.

Today, RAK produces a huge number of pharmaceuticals for Africa and the Middle East, while at the same time fostering the building of luxury hotels to take advantage of the good weather, and has also seen its technology and service sectors grow significantly.

The sheik came to our dinner for him in California one night. He brought his daughter with him and was happy to meet a small group of our friends who were happily surprised that he preferred to be addressed as "Saud" rather than "Your Highness." He didn't seem fazed at all when Gail stood up and announced, "Saud, I'm going to have to ask you to do something you may not have ever done before. I'm going to ask you to pick up your plate and go serve yourself at the buffet." He served himself plenty (and loved the food). It was truly a memorable evening for us all, and Saud regaled us with thoughts about the bad "neighborhood" he lived in—across the Strait of Hormuz from Iran and just around the corner from both Afghanistan and Iraq. He truly understands the risks his small country faces every day from these potential "bullies" but knows that he must work daily to achieve his vision for his people.

As the events in the first quarter of 2026 in Iran unfolded, everything Saud told us that night took on new meaning. And, having seen the Strait of Hormuz from the vantage point of his country, I knew what a choke point it would be for the conflict.

I came to know **Frank Fertitta** in my role as dean, as he was a proud alum of USC and our business school. He and his brother, Lorenzo, had taken over the running of the family chain of Las Vegas casinos/hotels that was started by their father in 1976.

In 2001, they took a risk and founded Zuffa LLC, the parent company of the Ultimate Fighting Championship—a mixed martial arts business coming out of Brazil. The American market was not particularly knowledgeable of this sport, and the risk was that a fledgling business would fail outside those markets where the fans knew it. Even riskier, the brothers were moving out of their core competence—that of running local casinos and hotels. The failure of UFC could cause them to take their eye off the ball of their main business as well as cause a diverting of capital and manpower. Whenever you do this, you run the risk of destroying what you've worked so hard to build up.

Frank considers himself a true entrepreneur and because of that, he did not think that the risks would outweigh the rewards. They set about educating the public about the sport and building it into an international one. It was an uphill climb, but adoption by young males gave them the impetus they needed. The sport and UFC specifically began to gain traction and grow. And by the time they sold Zuffa in 2016, it was worth $4 billion to them!

Again, the risk was significant and took time to mitigate. The reward, however, was even greater, so it truly was worth what they went through to build the sport. A little of Frank's successes accrued to me as we worked together in partnership to build a wonderful undergraduate instruction facility—Fertitta Hall stands as a cornerstone for the Marshall School in proud recognition of the success of UFC.

**Building something new is always a risk—but the rewards can be great.**

As one of founding fathers of Sandler O'Neill, **Fred Price** had his life and career altered on September 11, 2001, when his offices at the World Trade Center were destroyed by a terrorist-controlled airplane. He and one of his partners, Jimmy Dunne, happened to be out of the building that day and survived the attack, but they were the remaining partners who had to try to comfort and assist the families of their lost employees and they had to try to put their company back together again.

I will never forget their joint talk during Parents' Weekend at the Marshall School some years later where they reflected emotionally on what transpired that day and later that year. They split the tasks ahead of them—Jimmy tried to keep the business running and Fred worked with the families of their deceased employees, speaking at over thirty-five funerals. It had been well chronicled how they did this and how they were the role models for many firms that met with devastation that fateful day.

The first thing they did was to send paychecks to the families, covering the next four months' salaries of those employees, so the family could mourn and not worry in the short term about finances. In addition, they extended the health insurance for five years and later ten so they could have comfort and protection there. Finally, they committed to paying all tuition for the children of these employees who had perished.

They rebuilt their company, took care of the families of those they lost, and ultimately sold it in 2019. What they did during the few months after 9/11 defined the character of their company for the remainder of its existence. Yet, every time I talked with Fred Price, longtime member of our Marshall board about the incident, tears came to his eyes as he discussed it. He has never forgotten.

My final lesson about risk management came to me from one of our great American heroes and one you have probably never heard of. His name was **Walter Ehlers**, and he is one of the few awarded the Congressional Medal of Honor for his valiant efforts during the World War II invasion of Europe—D-Day on June 6, 1944, in Normandy, France.

Walt joined a group of us as we were going to tour the battlefields of Normandy. He was a soft-spoken, older man when we met him, and he began to open up about his story as we walked the beaches of Omaha and Utah and the hills above them.

The Medal of Honor is the highest military recognition our country can bestow on its servicepeople, and after Walt told his story, it was clear why he was a recipient. He was a sergeant in the United States Army on that fateful day as he and his team rode the landing ships to the shores of France. As he explained it, "My job was to get twelve men across that beach, up that hill, and into the French countryside." And as we know, the obstacles to that job were monumental—German machine gun nests, heavy artillery positions, daunting hills from which the enemy soldiers could rain down fire on the advancing troops.

As the fronts of the landing ships dropped, the American soldiers—many of them seasick from the ride across the channel—jumped into the shallow water and headed to shore. The first obstacle was a sandbar that had deep water between it and the shore—the geared-up, top-heavy soldiers fell upside down in that water from the initial sandbar; some perished before they even put their feet on solid ground. Walt pulled one up by his collar and saved his life, right out of the boat.

As the day progressed, Walt moved his band of twelve into the cracks on the cliff and up to the top. By nightfall, they were through the front lines and into the fields behind them. In the next days, a German machine gun nest pinned them down and they were unable to move. Sergeant Ehlers left his men, circled behind the enemy outpost, and took them out so he and his men could move further into the countryside.

Walt described D-Day to us in vivid detail. When asked what one thing stood out all those years later, he quickly responded, "The noise—it was as loud as anything I have ever heard. Ships and ground artillery shooting at each other; the air power in the skies; machine gun and small caliber weapon fire; the yelling of soldiers. The first five minutes of the movie *Saving Private Ryan* probably replicated it as close as anything."

He explained how the United States treats Medal of Honor recipients, honorably and respectfully. He still found it difficult to accept that when he walked through the halls of the Pentagon, four-star generals would come to a halt and salute him. "I am but a sergeant from Kansas," he would say.

He shared all of his experiences with us in a very humble manner, making it sound as if he was just there to do his job. He hated to answer the question as to how many enemy soldiers he killed. It was all about the men in his squad and how they scrambled for safety for days.

Walt left us is 2014, but I will never forget the lesson he taught us by his actions:

**Sometimes, you must take risks to take care of those around you. In doing so, stay humble, as you are one of many.**

Inevitably in life, even the most well-conceived and adroitly executed plan of risk management cannot anticipate every trapdoor or patch of poison ivy. My own life, as you have seen in these pages, has been filled with blessings galore and the lessons learned from hundreds of friends, colleagues, and sometimes just passing acquaintances. There have been lessons too from disappointments.

After I spent twelve years as dean at the Marshall School leading some six thousand students and five hundred faculty and staff, the USC front office, run by an interim president, decided to dismiss me. The stated reason was "necessary to repair campus culture after a series of embarrassing scandals." The student newspaper reported on the basis of unnamed sources that I was dismissed after the administration reviewed ten years' worth of complaints against Marshall faculty and staff that included "allegations of racial and gender discrimination and being a hostile workplace." USC administrators never explained to me or the public the reasons for my dismissal. But they did offer me the chance to remain dean for another year and the opportunity to collect the remaining three years of salary under my contract. I declined the offer, opting for transparency over secrecy and criticizing the administration's habitual practice of paying off a disgraced campus gynecologist and a rogue medical school dean with lucrative packages in return for nondisclosure agreements.

I had not seen the axe coming my way but was gratified when many members of the USC community—from trustees to students—objected to my ouster. The outcry forced the university to allow a team of faculty and staff (and me) to review ten years' worth of files in the Office of Equity and Diversity. There were about fifty-eight cases over ten years, none of them involving accusations of misconduct on my part. In more than 75 percent of cases, the files showed I had never been notified that a complaint had been filed. In the rare cases where I was looped into the process, the university's legal and HR people handled the situation according to their protocols.

You learn something, of course, from darker moments like this one or when all your risk calibration runs afoul. In my case, a good number of people came to my aid, and I will never forget their advocacy for me. Nor can I overlook those fair-weather birds who clucked a lot but didn't do much to actually help.

One of the university's trustees, **Ming Hsieh**, a hugely accomplished entrepreneur, stood up at a meeting and said that he was perplexed that a university already reeling from several public relations scandals would further tarnish its reputation by treating someone with my history the way I was being treated. Ming read all the documentary "evidence" in the files, including a report from a law firm hired by the university to review the situation, and he found "no evidence of sexual or aging discrimination at the Marshall School or by Dean Ellis." Instead, there was a track record anyone could be proud of: The graduate school had achieved by 2018 the highest ever ranking in the Bloomberg Survey of Best B-Schools—No. 14—while the undergraduate business program consistently maintained a top ten ranking, ultimately becoming number one. Female students were comprising 52 percent of the 2020 MBA class, and we had among the highest percentage of underrepresented minorities of any major business school in the country.

Ming and I had never been particularly close friends up to that point, but rather respectful acquaintances. His actions showed his belief that he was taking a stand not for me personally but for what he felt was right. I will never forget that, and I consider Ming a great friend today.

Another leader who supported me was **Lloyd Greif**, a self-made banker who had given generously to USC, solicited gifts for the school, and worked hard on its behalf. Upset by the irrational way the situation was being handled, Lloyd put himself out on a limb with letters to management, with responses to the media, and as organizer of a rally for me. Again, I came to understand he was fighting not for me but for what he believed in—for what he saw as right. I have said many times since then that if I'm ever facing a belligerent in a dark alley, Lloyd is the man I want right by my side.

As disappointed as I was with the unceremonious way I left USC, I have no regrets. I left the business school better than I found it and enjoyed virtually every minute of my time there. Life without risk doesn't exist, of course.

**Questions Relative to Risk, Vision, and Responsibility:**

- Have you ever been in a situation where you had to take a risk, and what did you do? Would you have done anything differently?
- Can you verbalize a vision for your life, career, or company that you are comfortable with implementing?
- When it comes time for you to take full responsibility for your actions or decisions, are you prepared to do so?
- What will it take for you to be ready if you are not already?

# Chapter 9

# The Fifth Decade

## *Giving Back*

In the last chapter, I told you about the paper that I wrote at Harvard Business School for Professor Gordon Marshall in the spring of 1970, answering the question "Where will you be in forty years and how did you get there?" I had divided my future into four distinct decades. Looking back now, I certainly would not have stopped my life at age sixty-two, as that paper read—that was back in the day when people actually retired at sixty-five. Today, I would add a fifth decade to those four, one that I never would have foreseen all those many years ago.

The fifth decade would be one of servant leadership—giving back to our community and to those less fortunate. I think that as we all gain wisdom and the ability to share, we should take it upon ourselves to do so. And there are so many ways that it can be done.

I personally never considered myself as philanthropic until I came into the academic world at the age of fifty. Oh sure, I had served on boards of nonprofit entities, but I was thinking they just wanted money, and maybe an idea or two, from me. And I always thought it was just something I should do, even though it took valuable time away my family and me. And then it came into focus: It IS something I should do—for the benefit of those various stakeholders.

At USC, we talked to our students early in their college careers about giving back to their communities. We had their fraternity and sorority experiences interwoven with philanthropic causes. And, as I said many times to students to drive the concept home, and it applies to us all, "When you are young, you have more time than money, and when you are old, you have more money than time." So very true. As students, they could be very philanthropic by sharing their time. They really were amazing in doing so, too. Collectively, they taught me great lessons.

As an example, USC's students would go to five of the surrounding elementary schools and read to the students. Our students recognized the value of reading as critical to childhood development. Amazing how good they felt when they returned to campus after a day with young kids who may not have had the opportunity to learn the joy of reading in their home life.

The professor who taught me the most about giving back was **Adlai Wertman**, our professor of social entrepreneurship. Adlai came in to see me one day, at the recommendation of our department chair, with an idea to bring social enterprise to the business school. He had been a successful investment banker in New York but felt there was way more to life than just making money. He had headed up a strong nonprofit in Los Angeles called Chrysalis, helping less fortunate people with job readiness and paid transitional employment, but wanted to take the concept of social entrepreneurship to the classroom.

Not only did I think we should hire Adlai, but we HAD to hire Adlai. It was that important to our students' education that we do so. He ultimately not only taught courses on social entrepreneurship, but also established the Brittingham Social Enterprise Lab, where students could be mentored in strong business skills to build careers in social impact businesses. It was a resounding success, completely attributable to Adlai and his vision for his students, and it set USC Marshall apart from other business schools. He taught me to take a chance, and how to succeed in doing so.

A project Adlai had his students work on was truly a game changer in scope: They worked with a foundation in the agricultural central California town of Arvin, population nineteen thousand. The population was almost entirely Latino, and nearly everyone worked in the fields or in processing, also mostly done in the field.

The project focused on the health of the workers who came home every day with boots and clothes covered in pesticides—sometimes the crop dusters flew right over them while they were working! Bringing that into the home exposed the rest of their families—spouses, kids, grandparents. Adlai's students spent days with the families, in their homes and the fields, and on weekends—just to see how they lived.

Once they understood the lifestyles, the students worked on designing marketable products that could be purchased by the farmworkers that could address the issue. All of this was presented to the residents, with the products then being redesigned and a business plan created around them!!

Additionally, the students did other projects for the town, figuring out jobs that could be created, as well as how the town might handle the annual movement of the itinerant workers, who would leave after the harvest season. All of this to benefit a small town—I sat in on the presentations to the town leaders, and they were just astonished at the creativity and thoughtfulness of the students. Very meaningful and applicable.

One USC student, **Zach Dell**, worked hard for the last two years of his undergraduate program trying to figure out how to get waterless toilets to all the small villages of India. He combined his newly acquired business acumen with the technical smarts of some engineering students to design these toilets, and he then flew to India numerous times to see how he might accomplish his lofty goal. I had great respect for his vision and for the way he approached the opportunity.

As Gandhi had said, "Good sanitation is more important than independence." And Indian Prime Minister Modi had committed a huge piece of his budget to ending defecating in the open by 2019. With over 750 million people in India lacking the appropriate indoor sanitation, Zach knew he was onto something. He and his partner were finalists for the 2017 Wrigley Sustainability Prize with their concept.

They founded a company named Sqwatt, with the promise to deliver low-cost sanitation products to countries such as India. While I am not sure what happened after that, as it seemed to disappear from the internet, the idea had great merit and, for a number of years, Zach worked hard on it.

Another student, **Alexander Duong**, founded his company because he wanted to create products that were gut friendly and from a supply chain that was good for people and for the planet. He felt that the stores were full of snack foods with harmful ingredients coming from supply chains that actively harmed the environment.

Fair & Square, the company Alex founded, has gluten-free, dairy-free, top fourteen allergen-friendly snacks, carried in retail outlets such as Whole Foods, Sprouts, Erewhon, and Thrive, as well as Amazon. More importantly, he has agreements with his suppliers—the farmers—that he will stand behind them and be fair. Finally, he has set up wholesale partnerships with Uber, Goop, Gap, and Open AI. They also have registered dietitians working with the company, creating more inclusive snacks. Keep up the good work, Alex!

At the same time as I was learning how to give back from my students and professors, I was learning it from my own family. My mother-in-law, **Mary Galvin**, is truly one of the most philanthropic individuals I have ever met. She had the wherewithal to do whatever she wanted, knew how best to use that, and then did. In one particular phase of her life, she had played the violin in the Illinois State Symphony orchestra, which led her to a lifelong love of the instrument. When she finally could, she opted to buy exceptionally high-quality violins, and she set up a foundation that would loan them to up-and-coming artists—people who would ultimately play them as star soloists. These now world-class musicians, such as Midori and Joshua Bell, had the use of an equally world-class instrument to develop and perfect their ability to perform. The founding of the Stradivarius Society was truly a game changer in the violin world, as burgeoning young musicians now had access early in their careers to the best instruments ever made, long before they really, if ever, could afford one. Perfect music made by the best to play the violin, with the best ones ever made, allowed audiences to hear what they might otherwise never have heard—music played the way the composer wrote it.

My wife, Gail, has always been involved in philanthropies and joined her mother in contributing violins to the society. Ultimately, her sister would join that effort as well. The apple had not fallen too far from the tree.

Gail's two brothers have also made significant contributions to the philanthropic world. **Christopher Galvin** has been involved at his alma mater, Northwestern University, as a member of the board of trustees for many years, giving of his time, ideas, and funds to help them build a renowned academic institution. Professors have shared with me how he has helped them think through problems, looking for acceptable solutions.

Brother **Michael Galvin** has led a very "give back" life. After practicing law, he was named as assistant secretary of commerce for industry and security in the George H. W. Bush administration—this type of work is a labor of love for one's country. Calculating how much money one makes in a job like this is a little daunting, as the salaries are low and the hours are long—and consequently the hourly wage is pretty low. Yet it is truly a philanthropic gesture, of great significance, to the United States.

Michael gives of his time every year, taking wounded veterans skiing on the slopes of Vail, Colorado, whenever he can. He has given them purpose as well as a physical outlet that enables them to accomplish something that they may not have ever thought they could achieve—skiing down a difficult ski run. And in addition to giving of his time to the veterans in his hometown, he has also stepped up to be the chair of the board of trustees at the Illinois Institute of Technology—a real donation of significant time, as it has been a total turnaround from its structural financial deficit, while it is uncompromising in its 135-year purpose-driven mission to elevate the underrepresented, socioeconomically disadvantaged student population. He has put his philanthropic entrepreneurship skills to work everywhere he goes and lives the life of a volunteer.

**Greg Hillgren** of Rancho Santa Fe, California, has a daughter whose firstborn son was born with a physical affliction that is very rare and possibly uncurable. Since the day JW was born, Greg has devoted himself to his grandson's issues, from traveling around the world and learning as much as he can from doctors who may or may not understand them, to sponsoring seminars where these doctors can come together to share their knowledge of the disease. He and his family have single-handedly worked as hard as they can to make the little guy's life, and that of many others in a similar situation, one that is long and wonderful. This is not just about time/ideas/money, but about love and passion.

Greg has demonstrated this passion previously with his work on behalf of Navy SEALs and all veterans through the Patriots Initiative—identifying and evaluating organizations devoted to supporting our veterans—as well as through his community's Rancho Santa Fe Foundation. He is relentless in his ability and desire to be a servant leader, all the experiences of which taught him how to try to find a cure his grandson's disease. We need more Gregs in the world.

In my time at USC, I met so many who were willing to support the school that they had attended and the students who were fortunate to be there, at that moment and in the future. Many students would achieve admission yet not know how they could afford to attend the university they had worked so hard to get into. Because of that, graduates were more than willing to support these students with scholarships—some 63 percent of those matriculating to USC were able to garner some funding that allowed them to attend. For me, raising funds for scholarships was by far the easiest of all causes; many had worked hard to get through the university and were now willing to give such that those behind them did not have to work or worry about how to pay next semester's tuition, and could just go to school and learn.

Regardless of why we are philanthropic, we ALWAYS feel better when we do something that helps others. As difficult as we think our lives can be, there is always someone who is having a more difficult time than we are and who needs our support.

In early 2025, in my Southern California environs, two significant wildfires took place, started on the very same night. Some thirteen thousand structures were burned, and thousands were out of their homes, which were either fully or partially destroyed by the wind-fanned flames. It was devastating to see the damage done in these two neighborhoods, knowing that people would be struggling for years to come before they could return to their homes, schools, shops, and restaurants—before their tight-knit communities would thrive again.

It had been amazing to see the outpouring of support for those who lost literally everything in the fires—people opening their homes, donating clothing now and probably furniture later, donating funds to support ongoing lives. We, for example, were asked by our daughter if we might be able to house our granddaughter's sewing teacher, who had been burned out of her apartment, in our guesthouse—we were more than happy to do so. She had to flee her apartment so quickly that she took only one change of clothes and her sewing machine—how she makes her living. That was ALL she could save. How could we not take her in, when we had the ability to do so? We have always said, "When you can, you do."

A group of teenaged girls from surrounding communities set up places where people could donate food, clothing, necessities—all to help their friends who had been displaced. . . . A teacher founded a nonprofit where donors could support the schools that had been burned out. . . . Food banks were open nonstop to take in food for people out of their homes. The Los Angeles community opened their homes, their wallets and purses, their schools to bring as much relief as they could to those unfortunate families. There are so very many ways that people can find to give back, and they are making it happen. It will be a long road, but help is there every step of the way.

My fifth decade in this life will find much of my time and effort being devoted to helping these less fortunate—most of whom I will never meet—get their lives back and be able to forge ahead. It will be the ultimate giveback, with the ultimate reward of knowing I have made a difference.

So, there you have it, a journey of many insights and lessons, some from those you would expect, like family, and some from those you never would guess, like JFK and students. I wanted to share these insights, as hopefully they will help those who read this to become better partners, parents, siblings, children, bosses, employees, and thought producers. We are all a product of our surroundings and our experiences. I definitely am that and, in my late stages of life, just wanted to share what I have gone through so that others might avoid mistakes I have made or amplify on good strides I have made. It is my giveback to you, the reader, with a thanks for listening, learning, and loving.

# Acknowledgments

As I finish this manuscript, I am well aware of the many people along the way who taught me great lessons but were not mentioned in the book. Some of you, knowing I was writing this, asked if there would be an entire chapter devoted to them!!! You were crushed when I had to tell you that you wound up on the cutting-room floor, and for that I am sorry.

I want to firstly thank both Chuck Crisafulli, a very accomplished writer who helped me get this launched and taught me a lot about writing, and Bruce Sanford, who helped me polish it and get it across the finish line. The book would never have happened without you two.

My family and friends have been so important to me throughout my life, and this book is dedicated to them. They pulled me through the dark days, and there were a few of them, and they celebrated with me during the great days that far outnumbered the dark ones. It has been a wonderful ride—when students ask me what decisions I might go back and change, I have to honestly answer them that I would change nothing. If I had changed anything, I would not be here today, writing this.

Every dark day is a learning experience for the next bright day, and we must look at it like that. Always look on the positive side and you will get through the dark days much faster. Devote yourself to your family, friends, and faith, and you will overcome most obstacles.

Finally, stay healthy. It sure helps you mentally to get up in the morning without the aches and pains of a physical nature. You can then focus on making it a great day, and you will.

**My Shoutouts to You Who Made a Difference but Did Not Make the Book:**

***The Early Years—***

Big H, Sol Singer, Roehl, Skinnae, Redman, Peter H., James, Scott, the Dears, Willy, the classroom teachers: Stoll, Form, and Telly

***The Boston Years—***

B/, Flandou, Chip, KCF, DSS, KQ, Otto, JFR, Fienning, Marshall, and Richie M'Tucci

***The Broadway Years—***

PMH, Mo, Woot, PK, PRJ, the Rock, O, Rhea, Mama D, Charlie, Gordo, Max, JC, Conrad, Walt, and MK

***The Hub Years—***

Shark, Jackson, Cindy, Modic, Bernards, Elliott, and Lawson

***The San Diego Years—***

JR, Frank, Barb, and Perri

***The Austrian Years—***

SJT, LDB, Jack, Joni and Kathleen, Herbie, and Peter, Leigh Ann and Bill

***The Indian Guide Years—***

Carlos, Les, Alan, Bo, Para, Tom and Bob

***The Entrepreneurial Years—***

JST, AJ, Carol, Norman, Suzanne, Rhea, the Eagles: MAM, WHB

***The YPO/WPO/CEO Years—***

Bruce, Chip, WP, Alpert, Omar, DK, Bobby, Steve, Mr. Coffey, Otto, Flury, Gadbois, the Romanian, Mayor Dee, Alison, Keith, Buddy T., and all my Forum mates

***The Redwood Years*—**
PJF, OMM, Quinn, Tex, Dwight, the Steves, the SEALs, Hacker, and all the Angels

***The Committee Years (Decades)*—**
EMW, JPS, Elliott, PCM, and interns JST and Carson

***The Board Years*—**
Jane and Cathie, Spellings, Hooper, Martin, Gitlin, Kevin, the Armours, Roye, JTodd, Brent, JGB, Debbie and Jeff, Mike and David, Kash, AndyW, Gabe

***The Coffee Group*—**
Petey, DC, Mark, Bill, Brad, Casey, Scotty, Jack, Colin, and Popo (finally)

***The Later Years*—**
Caswell, PWalker, Dr. Joe, Marc V, Lisa, Shep, the whole Murphy clan

***And, finally, the Trojan Years*—**
Beth, Dan, Tim, MO, Nancy, Lopesy, Gregg, Sunny, Hag, Muller, Kevin, Suryan, MD and the Seattle Gang, Warren, Nandini, Courtney, E, Rachel, Guille, CY, Hopper, Jan and Cynthia, Tito and Michael

And to the twenty-four thousand Trojans who have diplomas with my signature on them—you REALLY made and are making a difference . . . and for that I thank you profusely!!!

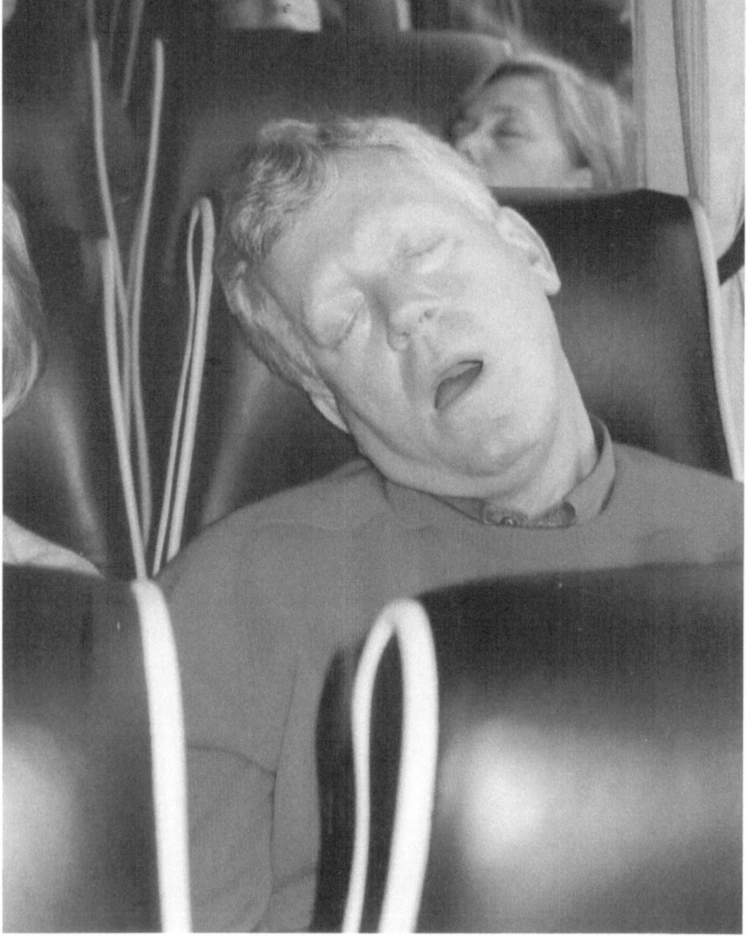

# Index

Photo insert images are indicated by *p1, p2, p3*, etc.

www.ingramcontent.com/pod-product-compliance
Ingram Content Group UK Ltd.
Pitfield, Milton Keynes, MK11 3LW, UK
UKHW040745171026
9277IPUK00008B/8

9 781493 096084